LA FUENTE

IBEROAMERICAN JOURNAL FOR CHRISTIAN WORLDVIEW

VOL. 5 | NO. 1, 2025

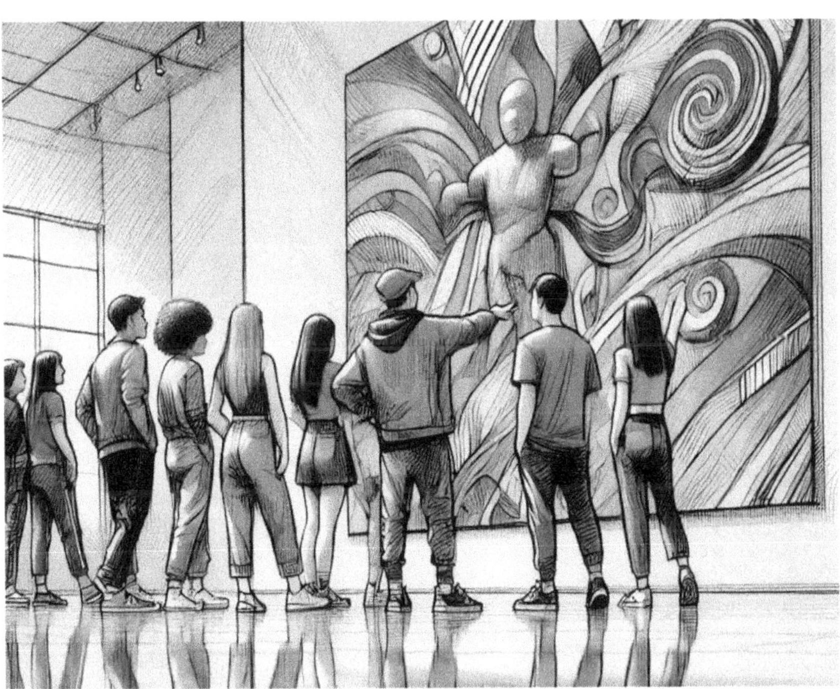

THE ARTS & CULTURE

LA FUENTE

IBEROAMERICAN JOURNAL FOR CHRISTIAN WORLDVIEW

VOL. 5 | NO. 1, 2025

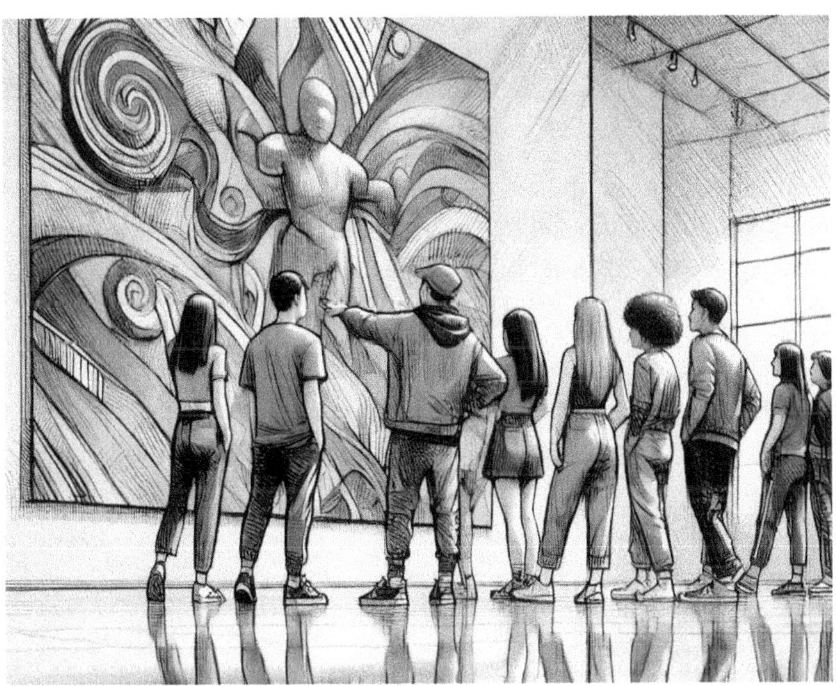

LAS ARTES Y LA CULTURA

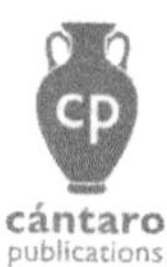

cántaro
publications

cantaroinstitute.org

Published by Cántaro Publications, a publishing imprint of the Cántaro Institute, Jordan Station, ON.

Journal design by Steven R. Martins

Translation and Editing by Steven R. Martins

Library & Archives Canada
ISBN 978-1-998711-16-1

Printed in the United States of America

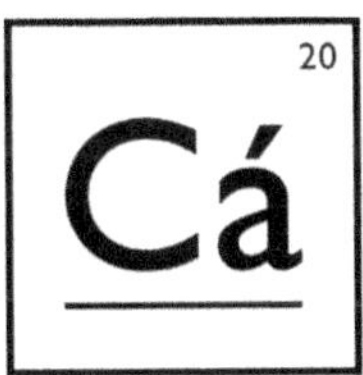

ABOUT THE CÁNTARO INSTITUTE

Inheriting, Informing, Inspiring

The Cántaro Institute is a reformed evangelical organization committed to the advancement of the Christian worldview for the reformation and renewal of the church and culture.

We believe that as the Christian church returns to the fount of Scripture as her ultimate authority for all knowing and living, and wisely applies God's truth to every aspect of life, her missiological activity will result in not only the renewal of the human person but also the reformation of culture, an inevitable result when the true scope and nature of the gospel is made known and applied.

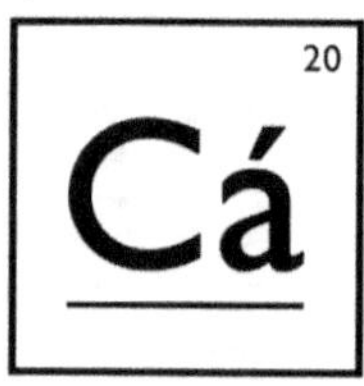

Editorial

by Cántaro Institute

NOW ENTERING its fifth year, *La Fuente: The Iberoamerican Journal for Christian Worldview* has become a widely read and respected resource in both English and Spanish, thanks to the faithful contributions of our writers and the ongoing support of ministry partners of the Cántaro Institute.

We are pleased to announce a recent contractual agreement with Logos Bible Software, which entails the inclusion of *La Fuente* in their Pre-Publication offerings. This means that every issue, if successfully funded—from the inaugural volume to the present and into the future—will be added to Logos' journal collection and made accessible to readers around the world. Alongside *La Fuente*, several titles from our publishing imprints, Paideia Press and Cántaro Publications, will also be featured in the Logos Pre-Pub catalogue. If you haven't already done so, we invite you to pre-order these titles to help ensure their funding and inclusion in Logos' growing library of theological and philosophical resources.

We also celebrate the recent addition of Ryan Lauterio to the Cántaro Institute as Associate for Christian Art & Aesthetics. A multi-award-winning artist, educator, and founder of The Maker Institute and Made Makers, Lauterio brings with him a deep commitment to the integration of art, theology, and aesthetics under the lordship of Christ. His appointment is marked by a contribution to this present issue of *La Fuente*, as well as several recorded lectures now available on our website.

This year's issue, *The Arts & Culture*, explores the breadth of the Cántaro Institute's worldview instruction with a focused engagement in the aesthetic (artistic) sphere. It opens with "The Don Quixotic Syndrome" by Institute founder Steven R. Martins—a compelling philosophical and theological allegory diagnosing modern man's spiritual condition as one of self-imposed delusion. Like Cervantes' tragic knight, the autonomous man lives in denial of reality, constructing a false world of his own making while suppressing the truth revealed by God. Tracing this madness through the intellectual history of Western civilization—from ancient Greek dualism and Scholasticism to Enlightenment autonomy and postmodern emotionalism—Martins argues that only the Reformation's biblical framework of Creation, Fall, and Redemption can break the spell. True freedom, he contends, is not found in autonomy but in submission to the Lordship of Christ, who alone restores our vision of the world as it truly is.

Following this is "Art and the Cultural Mandate" by Ryan Eras, headmaster of Niagara Classical Academy, which explores the biblical foundation for art within the framework of the cultural mandate. Eras demonstrates that creativity is a central expression of mankind's identity as image-bearers of God. Art, when rightly ordered, glorifies God by symbolically revealing truth and beauty grounded in the created order. Drawing from Scripture, Reformed thinkers, and Christian artists, the article critiques both the nihilism of modern art and the sentimental retreat of much contemporary Christian art, calling instead for faithful, Spirit-filled creativity rooted in reality. Rather than mimic secular forms or retreat into clichés, Christians are urged to reclaim the arts with excellence, honesty, and theological integrity.

Next is a special republication of Dr. Calvin G. Seerveld's out-of-print address, "Human Responses to Art: Good, Bad, and Indifferent." A close friend of the Institute, Seerveld challenges Christians to move beyond shallow or overly intellectualized reactions to art and to cultivate imaginative, Spirit-led responses grounded in biblical discernment. Delivered at Dordt College in 1981, the lecture critiques common misperceptions of art—as mere stimulation, technical display, paraphrasable message, or dissectible concept—and instead calls for a Christian aesthetic rooted in the symbolical nature of artistic work. Art, Seerveld argues, is an allusive and crafted object that must be "read" imaginatively and contextually. With insights drawn from Revelation, philosophy, and Scripture, Seerveld reminds us that our artistic perception must be shaped by a desire to honour Christ, discern truth, and engage culture redemptively.

Finally, the issue concludes with "A Call to True, Excellent, and Reformational Making" by Ryan Lauterio, founder of the Maker Institute and Made Makers, and newly appointed Associate for Christian Art and Aesthetics at the Cántaro Institute. In a culture saturated by design and artistic influence, Lauterio issues a timely and reformational challenge—Kuyperian in spirit—for Christians to reclaim the arts under the Lordship of Christ. Drawing on Scripture and voices like Seerveld, he warns of the consequences of neglecting the creative domain, where secular ideologies continue to distort truth and shape the cultural imagination. Christians, he urges, must respond as faithful image-bearers by cultivating excellence in art, design, and making—grounded in gratitude, theological clarity, and Spirit-filled discernment. With courage, compassion, and craftsmanship, Christian artists are called to reflect God's glory, resist cultural falsehoods, and lead a generational movement rooted in truth, beauty, and the transformative power of the Gospel.

Altogether, we trust this rich collection of written contributions will be beneficial, edifying, and exhortative for readers seeking to live faithfully and distinctly Christian lives—particularly in the aesthetic (artistic) sphere.

Soli Deo Gloria.

Editorial

por el Cántaro Institute

AHORA EN SU quinto año, *La Fuente: Iberoamerican Journal for Christian Worldview* se ha convertido en un recurso ampliamente leído y respetado tanto en inglés como en español, gracias a las fieles contribuciones de nuestros escritores y al continuo apoyo de los colaboradores ministeriales del Cántaro Institute.

Nos complace anunciar un reciente acuerdo contractual con Logos Bible Software, que incluye la incorporación de *La Fuente* en sus ofertas de Pre-Publicación. Esto significa que cada número—desde el volumen inaugural hasta el presente y hacia el futuro—será agregado a la colección de revistas de Logos y estará disponible para lectores en todo el mundo, siempre que el proyecto reciba el financiamiento necesario. Junto con *La Fuente*, varios títulos de nuestras editoriales, Paideia Press y Cántaro Publications, también formarán parte del catálogo de Pre-Publicación de Logos.

Si aún no lo ha hecho, le invitamos a pre-ordenar estos títulos para ayudar a garantizar su financiación e inclusión en la creciente biblioteca de recursos teológicos y filosóficos de Logos.

También celebramos la reciente incorporación de Ryan Lauterio al Cántaro Institute como Asociado en Arte y Estética Cristiana. Galardonado artista, educador y fundador de The Maker Institute y Made Makers, Lauterio aporta un profundo compromiso con la integración del arte, la teología y la estética bajo el señorío de Cristo. Su nombramiento queda marcado por una contribución en el presente número de *La Fuente*, así como por varias conferencias grabadas que ya se encuentran disponibles en nuestro sitio web.

El número de este año, titulado *Las Artes y la Cultura*, explora la amplitud de la instrucción en cosmovisión del Cántaro Institute con un enfoque particular en la esfera estética (artística). Se abre con "El Síndrome de Don Quijote" del fundador del Instituto, Steven R. Martins—una alegoría filosófica y teológica que diagnostica la condición espiritual del hombre moderno como una de autoengaño. Al igual que el trágico caballero de Cervantes, el hombre autónomo vive en negación de la realidad, construyendo un mundo falso de su propia invención mientras suprime la verdad revelada por Dios. Martins rastrea esta locura a lo largo de la historia intelectual de la civilización occidental—desde el dualismo griego antiguo y la escolástica hasta la autonomía ilustrada y el emocionalismo posmoderno—y argumenta que solo el marco bíblico de la Reforma—Creación, Caída y Redención—puede romper el hechizo. La verdadera libertad, sostiene, no se encuentra en la autonomía, sino en la sumisión al señorío de Cristo, quien es el único que puede restaurar nuestra visión del mundo tal como es.

Le sigue "Arte y el Mandato Cultural" por Ryan Eras, director de Niagara Classical Academy, quien explora el fundamento bíblico del arte dentro del marco del mandato cultural. Eras demuestra que la creatividad es una expresión central de la identidad del ser humano como portador de la imagen de Dios. El arte, cuando está correctamente ordenado, glorifica a Dios al revelar simbólicamente la verdad y la belleza arraigadas en el orden creado. Basándose en la Escritura, pensadores reformados y artistas cristianos, el artículo critica tanto el nihilismo del arte moderno como la retirada sentimental del arte cristiano contemporáneo, y en su lugar, llama a una creatividad fiel y llena del Espíritu, enraizada en la realidad. En lugar de imitar las formas seculares o refugiarse en clichés, se insta a los cristianos a reclamar las artes con excelencia, honestidad e integridad teológica.

A continuación, se presenta una reedición especial del discurso fuera de circulación del Dr. Calvin G. Seerveld, "Respuestas Humanas al Arte: Buenas, Malas e Indiferentes". Amigo cercano del Instituto, Seerveld desafía a los cristianos a ir más allá de las reacciones superficiales o excesivamente intelectualizadas al arte y a cultivar respuestas imaginativas y guiadas por el Espíritu, enraizadas en el discernimiento bíblico. Entregado en Dordt College en 1981, el discurso critica concepciones comunes del arte—como mera estimulación, demostración técnica, mensaje parafraseable o concepto disectable—y en su lugar, aboga por una estética cristiana basada en la naturaleza simbólica del trabajo artístico. El arte, argumenta Seerveld, es un objeto elaborado y alusivo que debe ser "leído" imaginativamente y en contexto. Con ideas extraídas de Apocalipsis, la filosofía y la Escritura, Seerveld nos recuerda que nuestra percepción artística debe estar moldeada por el deseo de honrar a Cristo, discernir la verdad y comprometerse culturalmente de manera redentora.

Finalmente, el número concluye con "Un Llamado a una Obra Verdadera, Excelente y Reformacional", de Ryan Lauterio, fundador de The Maker Institute y Made Makers, y recientemente nombrado Asociado en Arte y Estética Cristiana del Cántaro Institute. En una cultura saturada de diseño e influencia artística, Lauterio lanza un llamado urgente y reformacional, de espíritu kuyperiano, para que los cristianos reclamen las artes bajo el señorío de Cristo. Apoyándose en la Escritura y en voces como la de Seerveld, advierte sobre las consecuencias de descuidar el dominio creativo, donde las ideologías seculares continúan distorsionando la verdad y moldeando la imaginación cultural. Lauterio exhorta a los cristianos a responder como portadores fieles de la imagen de Dios, cultivando la excelencia en el arte, el diseño y la creación, fundamentados en la gratitud, la

claridad teológica y el discernimiento lleno del Espíritu. Con valentía, compasión y destreza, los artistas cristianos son llamados a reflejar la gloria de Dios, resistir las falsedades culturales y liderar un movimiento generacional arraigado en la verdad, la belleza y el poder transformador del Evangelio.

En conjunto, confiamos en que esta rica colección de contribuciones escritas será de gran beneficio, edificación y exhortación para los lectores que buscan vivir vidas fieles y distintivamente cristianas—especialmente en la esfera estética (artística).

Soli Deo Gloria.

The Don Quixotic Syndrome

by Steven R. Martins

A Psychiatrist and his Patient

IT WAS A STORMY night when a patient stepped into his psychiatrist's office. The wind howled outside, and the rhythmic tapping of rain against the window filled the dimly lit room. He took his seat on the reclined chair, exhaled deeply, and fixed his gaze on the ceiling.

"It's good to see you again, doctor," he said, "I must say, the affliction persists. Perhaps you could help."

The psychiatrist, already settled in his swivel chair, notepad open and pen in hand, responded with the practiced calm of one who had heard it all before.

"And what is it that afflicts you?"

"The same as always, doctor. I see what no one else sees. I feel as if *I'm* the lunatic."

"And that is not your affliction?," the psychiatrist asked rhetorically, barely lifting his eyes from his notes. "We've discussed this before during your last visit. But since you are here, why don't you tell me again what you believe your affliction to be?"

"Why, I am afflicted by the lunacy of others!" the patient declared.

The psychiatrist leaned back. "And how so?"

The patient shifted in his seat, looking out at the window just across the room. "Take your secretary, for instance. Do you know what she said to me when I arrived?"

"I do not," the psychiatrist said, glancing up. "What did she say?"

"She said, 'It's pouring rain out there.'"

"And is it not pouring rain?"

"Of course not!" The patient gestured toward the window. "The sun is shining brilliantly. The sky is as clear as can be."

The psychiatrist considered him carefully, not even glancing at the window where he heard the rain patter. "And the drops of water on your jacket?"

"I must have been sweating profusely."

"The wet soles of your shoes?"

"A dog must have relieved itself by the entrance."

"And the sound of thunder rolling in the distance?"

"Oh, that?" The patient smirked. "You mean the never-ending construction on the streets?"

The psychiatrist sighed, jotting something in his notebook.

"You really don't care what I have to say, do you?" the patient asked.

The psychiatrist set his pen down. "Let me ask you this—why do you think you see things so differently from the rest of the world? Even when reality stares you in the face?"

The patient scoffed at the blatant remark, thought to himself for a moment and then responded. "So you think I'm the one with the problem.

But tell me, doctor—if the world is mad, does it not follow that the sane man will appear mad in their eyes?"

The psychiatrist studied him in silence.

The patient stood, straightened his jacket, and walked to the door. Before leaving, he glanced back. "Thanks, doc. You might want to get yourself checked out. You're just as much a loon as everyone else."

As the door clicked shut, the psychiatrist tapped his pen against the notepad, deep in thought. His gaze drifted to the bookshelf beside him, landing on a familiar title—*Don Quixote*. A knowing smile played at his lips.

"Ah," he murmured. "I know what to call this."

He flipped to a fresh page and, in bold capital letters, wrote:

DON QUIXOTIC SYNDROME

He circled the words with a red pen. "This is what I will call it," he mused. Then, with a faint smirk, he added, "He better not imagine away the bill that awaits him."

Don Quixote as an Allegory for the Autonomous Man

The above work of fiction illustrates the condition of the autonomous man—spiritually blind and ensnared in self-delusion, incapable of perceiving the truth even when faced with reality. In this respect, he bears a striking resemblance to Don Quixote, both seeing the world not as it is, but *as they imagine it to be.*

Don Quixote, along with his squire Sancho Panza, is widely recognized as one of the great literary figures in Western literature, a classic for all who speak the language of Miguel de Cervantes. However, beyond its comedic exterior, *Don Quixote* is a profound allegory of the fallen man in the world of God. Whether or not Cervantes intended it, his work serves as a remarkable depiction of the autonomous man—one who, rejecting the truth of God's revelation, constructs an illusory reality in defiance of the created order. Harold Bloom insightfully noted that *Don Quixote* is, at its core, more of a tragedy than a comedy. And what is the story of sinful man if not the greatest tragedy of all?[1]

Russian literary scholar Vladimir Nabokov, in his posthumously published lectures on *Don Quixote*, describes the protagonist before his self-imposed transformation:

> Before he dubs himself Don Quixote, his name is plain Quijada, or Quesada. He is a country gentleman, owner of a vineyard, master's house, and two acres of arable land; a good Catholic (who will later evolve a bad conscience); a tall, lanky gentleman around fifty... [And] the man Sancho Panza. Who is he? A laborer who had been a shepherd in his youth, and then, at one time, a beadle to a brotherhood. He is a family man but a vagabond at heart....[2]

Quixote and Sancho are not introduced as fantastical or surreal figures, but as ordinary men. And yet, as the story unfolds, they are afflicted with a peculiar madness, perceiving reality through a framework entirely disconnected from what actually is. This detachment from reality is the mark of the autonomous man. He lives and breathes in God's world, he knows the truth of all things in his heart of hearts (Rom. 1:18), but in his sinful heart he suppresses the truth, constructing in its place an illusion that does not at all comport with reality.

This tragic *delusion* is evident in today's world, as the autonomous man—believing himself indepen-

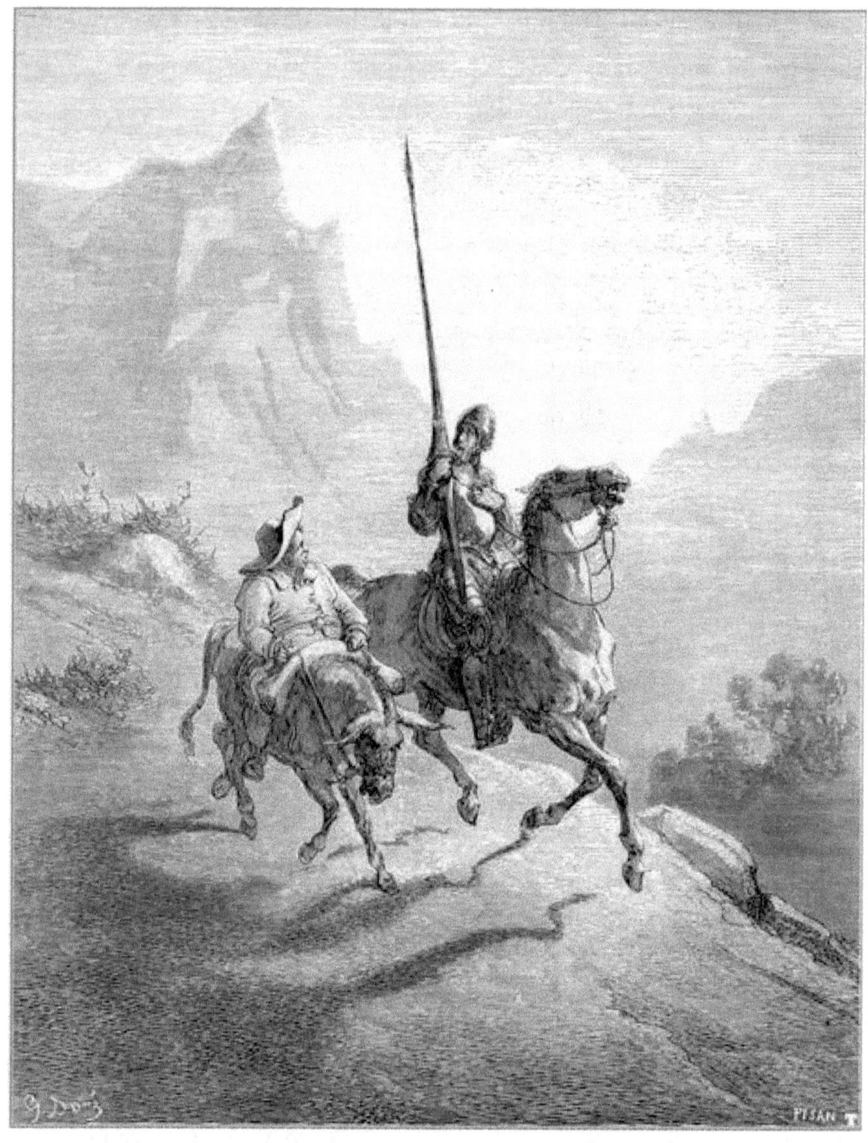

"Don Quixote and Sancho Setting Out" (1863) by Gustave Doré.

dent from God in every respect, and as thus being his own ultimate authority—rejects divine revelation in pursuit of redefining even the most fundamental aspects of reality. Consider, for example, a strikingly modern instance of this rebellion: During the U.S. confirmation hearing of Judge Ketanji Brown Jackson, Senator Marsha Blackburn posed a simple question: "Can you provide a definition for the word 'woman'?" One might expect an immediate and self-evident answer. Yet Jackson's response—"Can I provide a definition though? I can't. Not in this context, I'm not a biologist."—was no answer at all. A laughable moment perhaps, but this is not a comedy, this is a tragedy.[3]

We might ask, "Does sinful man truly believe his own illusions?" In light of this cited instance, did Judge Jackson genuinely *believe* that her refusal to define the word "woman"—on the grounds that she had no answer—was rooted in truth? At the surface, it seems so. It is, after all, the confession of the modern apostate. But in the depths of man's heart, man knows the illusion is a lie. Man's false world is nothing more than an artificial construct—a façade erected over reality, one that he must constantly uphold to stave off the crushing weight of truth. Or, to put it in more biblical terms, he must relentlessly *suppress* the truth (Rom. 1:18), forcing it down like a beach ball beneath the water, lest it break through the surface and shatter his delusion.

This is precisely the condition of Don Quixote. He lives by an illusion, fabricating a world in which he is a noble, chivalrous knight, where reality bends to fit his imagined grandeur.

Let no one dare suggest he is not a knight, and no one question his illusions—for they must not only be indulged but affirmed as true realities. Yet deep down, he does not fully believe in the reality of his own vision. Bloom observes:

> Does Don Quixote altogether believe in the reality of his own vision? Evidently he does not, particularly when he (and Sancho) is surrendered by Cervantes to the sadomasochistic practical jokes—indeed, the vicious and humiliating cruelties—that afflict the Knight and squire in part II.[4]

One particularly vivid example of this tension between illusion and reality is found in chapter 18 of *Don Quixote*. Nabokov summarizes the scene in which Quixote, gripped by "strange madness," mistakes two flocks of sheep, along with the dust they raise, for two mighty armies. In this scene, Sancho protests:

> "Sir," he said, "may I go to the devil if I see a single man, giant, or knight of all those that your grace is talking about. Who knows? Maybe it is another spell, like last night."[5]

Quixote, however, will hear none of it:

"How can you say that?" replied Don Quixote. "Can you not hear the neighing of the horses, the sound of trumpets, the roll of drums?"[6]

To which Sancho responds, bewildered:

"I hear nothing," said Sancho, "except the bleating of sheep."[7]

One would expect that Quixote would awaken to the absurdity of his illusion as he rides through the flock of sheep. Surely, with such overwhelming evidence against his belief, he would admit his madness. But no—he instead doubles down, blaming a sinister magician for his misfortune:

"This," said Don Quixote, "is the work of that thieving magician, my enemy, who thus counterfeits things and causes them to disappear. You must know, Sancho, that it is very easy for them to make us assume any appearance that they choose; and so it is that malign one who persecutes me, envious of the glory he saw me about to achieve in this battle, changed the squadrons of the foe into flocks of sheep."[8]

This is the condition of the autonomous man. He is confronted daily with the truth—everywhere he turns, reality testifies against him. Yet he cannot yield. He must persist in his delusion, no matter how overwhelming the evidence against him.[9] And in truth, there is only one true form of evidence—*God's evidence*—for whatever he may claim in his defense is nothing more than a distorted interpretation of what God has revealed in His created order. For the autonomous man, the irrationality of sin prevails over any appeal to reason, for his very faculties are enslaved to his rebellion. And herein lies the futility of seeking to *reason* the sinner into saving faith apart from the work of the Spirit of God. Does he not, like Don Quixote, have moments where he wavers, where he senses that something is terribly wrong with his illusion? Certainly. But these moments are fleeting, and his madness—his *foolishness*, as Scripture calls it (Ps. 14:1; Rom. 1:22)—is stronger than all else. As long as he remains autonomous, that is to say, in blatant rebellion to God and His law, his faculties will not serve the truth but instead will be bound to the suppression of it.

Thus, we are not merely dealing with intellectual error, but with the profound spiritual bondage of sin that afflicts the autonomous man. It requires nothing less than the sovereign grace of God to shatter the sinner's illusion, stripping away the falsehoods to which he so desperately clings. Only through the effectual working of the Spirit can man's mind be renewed, and only through the testimony of the living Word of God can his heart be turned from darkness to light. Until then, man, bound by his Don Quixotic syndrome, will continue to charge at windmills, convinced they are giants. He will persist in calling sheep an army, deaf to the sound of their bleating. In short, he will redefine reality itself to fit his self-made narrative much to his peril, even as all of creation testifies against him. And in the end, like Don Quixote, he will find that when his illusion finally collapses, there is nothing left—no action remaining except to die,[10] if he so chooses to not repent and surrender to God.

The Development of Western Thought

It would be difficult to argue that the "Don Quixotic" syndrome of man emerged in a vacuum, as though it arose "spontaneously" without rational explanation or logical causation. Rather, the Don Quixotic syndrome must be understood within a much broader context.

First and foremost, this Don Quixotic syndrome is a consequence of our first parents' sin. Their original transgression—the pursuit of radical autonomy, a desire to exist independently from God in every respect and to become gods—brought about not only the fallenness of the world (Gen. 3:17-19), evident in the pervasive realities of injustice, suffering, death, and decay, but also the corruption of mankind's fundamental orientation in life, particularly in the realm of thought (Jer. 17:9; Rom. 1:21-22; Eph. 4:17-18).

Given this intellectual distortion, it is prudent to examine the historical development of the thought of Western civilization. Put simply, fallen man's present state—that is, being afflicted with the Don Quixotic syndrome—is not without precedent, but is rather the culmination of centuries of philosophical and theological development rooted in false, antithetical presuppositions.

How might we span such a vast expanse of time while accurately encapsulating the historical development of Western thought? For starters, we must recognize that the intellectual history of the West is shaped by distinct worldviews—a worldview is a network of presuppositions that originate from the heart. In this sense, we could also say that the intellectual history of the West is shaped by fundamental *heart commitments* that influence man's thought and, consequently, the society in which he lives. As the late Dutch Christian philosopher Herman Dooyeweerd (1894–1977) observes in his seminal work, *The Roots of Western Culture*, these worldviews can be categorized into four fundamental ground-motives. Three of these are apostate in both structure (their presuppositions) and direction (that which is worshipped), while one alone is faithful in its structure (that is to say, it is correspondent to reality) and direction (oriented toward the worship of the one true God). These ground-motives are: (i) the Matter-Form scheme of Greek philosophy, (ii) the Grace-Nature scheme of medieval Scholasticism, (iii) the Freedom-Nature dichotomy of the Enlightenment, and (iv) the Creation-Fall-Redemption framework of the Reformation—the only one of the four ground-motives that is *not* apostate. Historically, the Creation-Fall-Redemption framework of the Reformation follows that of medieval Scholasticism, but to distinguish it clearly from the apostate ground

motives, I have placed it last. In the context of contemporary thought, the Freedom-Nature dichotomy is most pertinent; however, before proceeding, a proper understanding requires tracing the ideological progression that first led to it.

The Matter-Form Scheme of Greek Thought

It cannot be denied that ancient Greek civilization played a formative role in shaping the Western intellectual tradition. Among its most influential thinkers were Plato and Aristotle, whose Matter-Form dualism posited two distinct and irreconcilable realms: the world of *Matter*, in which we live, and the world of *Forms*, which exists beyond the material. Broadly speaking, this intellectual tradition regarded the material world as nothing more than a mere shadow of a higher, immutable reality. For instance, a horse in the material world was understood as an imperfect representation of an idealized "horse-ness" existing in the realm of *Forms*. The same could be said of beauty, it was understood as an imperfect representation of an idealized "beauty-ness" existing in the realm of *Forms*. And how did man supposedly come to know these *Forms*? According to Plato's doctrine of *anamnesis* (recollection), man's soul—before becoming confined within the material body—originated from the realm of *Forms* itself. Man does not learn something new, he merely recollects lost memories from before his incarnation. This dualism of Matter-Form permeated Greek culture, as Dooyeweerd explains:

> The Greek motive of *matter*, the formless principle of becoming and decay, was oriented to the aspect of movement in temporal reality. It gave Greek thought and all of Greek culture a hint of dark mystery which is foreign to modern thinking. The Greek motive of culture, on the other hand, was oriented to the cultural aspect of temporal reality ("culture" means essentially the free forming of matter). It constantly directed thought to an extrasensory, imperishable *form* of being that transcended the cyclical life stream.[11]

This fragmentation of reality, however, is not merely an intellectual error, but a direct consequence of man's fallen condition. The Fall (Rom. 1:18–25), in addition to introducing the curse of sin and death into the world, corrupted man's capacity for reason, resulting in a suppression of truth and an embrace of distorted perceptions of reality. The ancient Greek worldview exemplified this suppression in its philosophical framework—an early manifestation of mankind's misinterpretation of creation, one that failed to recognize the unity and coherence of God's order.

The Grace-Nature Scheme of Scholasticism

What followed the Greeks was a profound engagement between biblical revelation and Greek thought, shortly after the rise of Christianity. As the early church (particularly the patristics) grappled with questions of theology and philosophy, Greek categories increasingly shaped its intellectual framework. This engagement culminated in the medieval Scholastic tradition, most fully developed by Thomas Aquinas, which introduced the Grace-Nature scheme. Within this framework, reality was divided into two distinct realms: *Grace*, representing all that is sacred, and *Nature*, encompassing the fallen world, including Greek philosophy. Scholasticism maintained that *Grace* perfected *Nature*, yet the two remained fundamentally distinct.

This dualism posed an inherent theological problem: how could the divine and the profane be reconciled? While Scholasticism sought a synthesis, it failed to grasp the full depth of human depravity, treating sin as a mere weakness rather than a fundamental corruption of the heart. Aristotle and Plato, for all their philosophical brilliance, were pagans whose reasoning was inevitably tainted by the Fall. To assume that their insights could be harmonized with divine revelation *without consequential distortion* was to underestimate the radical effects of sin. Dooyeweerd critiques this attempt:

> Aristotle's Greek view of nature was pagan. Nevertheless, the Roman Catholic ground-motive of nature and grace sought to accommodate the Greek ground-motive to that of divine revelation. The scholastics argued that whatever was subject to birth and death, including human beings, was constituted of matter and form. God created all things according to this arrangement. As a *natural* being, for example, they held that a person consists of a "rational soul" and a "material body." Characterized by its capacity for thought, the rational soul was both the "invisible, essential form" of the body and an imperishable "substance" that could exist apart from the body... But this human "nature," which is guided by the natural light of reason, was not corrupted by sin and thus also does

not need to be restored by Christ. Human nature is only "weakened" by the fall. It continues to remain true to its innate "natural law" and possesses an autonomy, a relative independence and self-determination in opposition to the realm of grace of the Christian religion.[12]

Herein lies the fundamental flaw of Scholasticism: it treated natural reason as autonomous—that is, as neutral and independent—thereby downplaying the total corruption of sin. By asserting that reason was merely weakened rather than wholly fallen, Scholasticism laid the groundwork for a compartmentalized view of reality. This is most evident in the sacred-secular divide that persists in much of contemporary thought, where certain aspects of life are deemed "spiritual" and thus *private*, while others are considered "neutral" or "secular" and thus *public*. Such a dichotomy is incompatible with God's sovereignty and His rule over all things.

The Creation-Fall-Redemption Framework of the Reformation

What followed historically was the emergence of the Protestant Reformation, introducing a new ground-motive—the only one of the four that faithfully reflects reality. What the

Reformation did was expose the dangerous implications of Scholastic dualism, calling for a return to the absolute authority of Scripture (*Sola Scriptura*). The Reformers rejected the notion that human reason could function *autonomously* from divine revelation. Instead, they articulated a comprehensive, biblical framework: the Creation-Fall-Redemption ground-motive. This paradigm acknowledges that:

1. **Creation**—God created all things good, and the created order reflects His divine structure and purpose.

2. **Fall**—Sin has corrupted not only human nature but all aspects of reality, distorting relationships, institutions, and even the natural world.

3. **Redemption**—Christ's redemptive work extends beyond individual salvation to the restoration of the entire created order.

Unlike previous worldviews, this framework rejected the validity of dualistic thinking. There was no Matter-Form dualism, no Grace-Nature dualism, and therefore no sacred-sec-ular divide; all of life fell under the sovereign reign of Christ. This meant that philosophy, politics, science, and the arts were not to operate on the basis of autonomous human reasoning, but were to be subjected to, and reoriented according to biblical truth.

The Reformers, in essence, understood that the Fall had corrupted every aspect of human existence, and thus that it necessitated a comprehensive redemption. This was the rise of the Creation-Fall-Redemption framework as man's understanding of reality under the light of God's Word. But while figures like John Calvin and Martin Luther sought to purge Christian thought of its Scholastic entanglements, many who followed unwittingly reintroduced them through the back door. Consequently, though the implications of this ground-motive were genuinely transformative—fundamentally shaping, or rather, *reforming*, the trajectory of Western thought—it remained susceptible to intellectual compromise. This concession left it vulnerable to the counter-movement that soon emerged, one that sought to reject divine authority altogether.

The Freedom-Nature Dichotomy of the Enlightenment

The Enlightenment, emerging as a reaction against the Reformation, sought to reassert human autonomy by establishing a new ground-motive: the Freedom-Nature scheme. This worldview posited an irreconcilable tension between the deterministic laws of *Nature* and the ideal of human *Freedom*. Enlightenment thinkers envisioned the world (*Nature*) as a vast mechanistic system governed by immutable laws while simultaneously insisting on mankind's ability to transcend these constraints through reason and self-determination (*Freedom*).

However, this dichotomy proved inherently contradictory. If *Nature* is governed by fixed laws, how can man possess true *Freedom*? If all things are determined, how can autonomy exist? This unresolved tension led to a crisis in Western thought.

If we were to identify the dominant ground-motive of our culture today, it would undoubtedly be the Freedom-Nature scheme, now shaped more by Romanticism than by Rationalism. The failure of Enlightenment rationalism—its inability to satisfy mankind's existential and spiritual longings—paved the way for Romanticism, a movement that rejected cold empiricism in favor of emotion and imagination. Here, the quest for autonomy reached its zenith: man, liberated from the constraints of reason, sought to define reality on his own terms. The consequences are evident in modern thought—namely, the rejection of objective truth, the rise of radical subjectivism, and the dominance of emotionalism over rational discourse. How best to explain this other than René Descartes' "I think, therefore I am" has given way to "I *feel*, therefore I am."

Understanding Better the Don Quixotic Syndrome

The intellectual history of the West, in many respects, can be understood as the unfolding narrative of mankind's tragic rebellion against God and His creational order. From the dualisms inherent in Greek philosophy to the attempted synthesis of Scholasticism, to the Enlightenment's radical assertion of human autonomy, each reveals the consequences of an apostate heart. As Dooyeweerd astutely observed, the fundamental issue is not merely one of intellectual divergence but of profound spiritual significance:

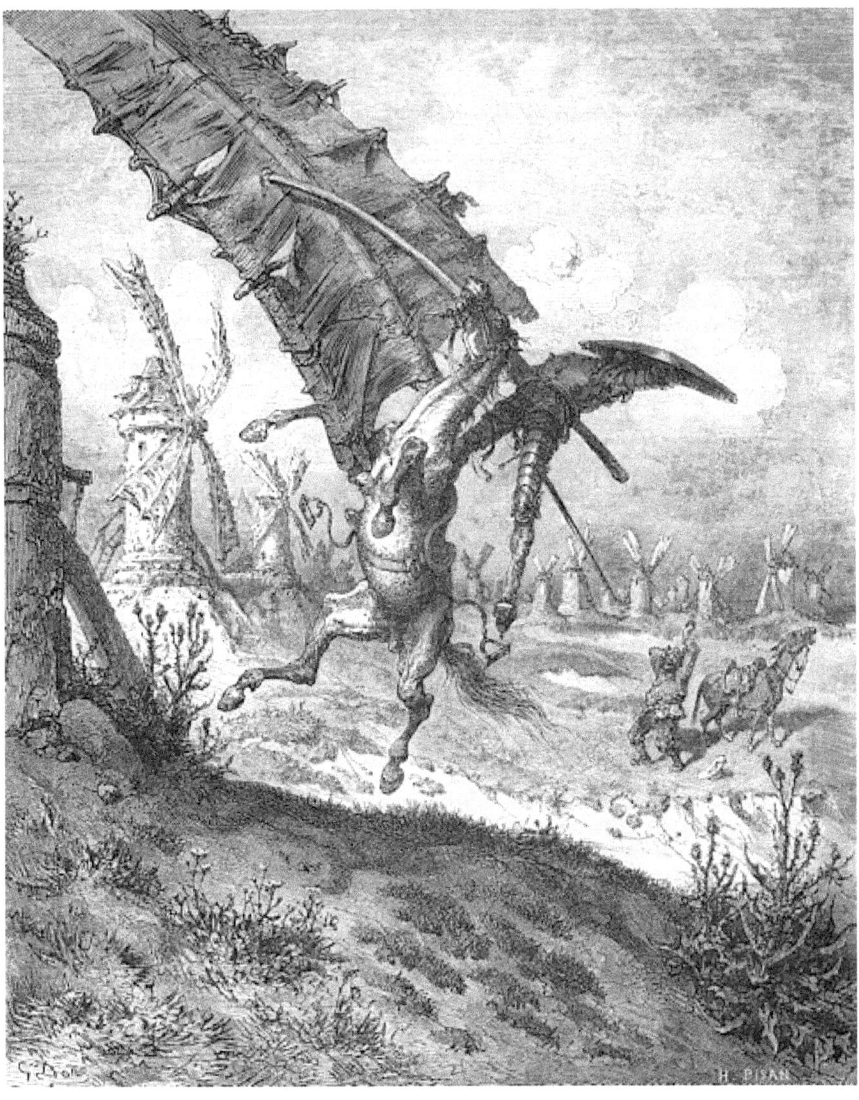

"Don Quixote and Windmill" (1863) by Gustave Doré.

It [all] issues from the religious root of our temporal life, namely, the heart, soul, or spirit of a person. Because of the fall into sin, the hearts of human beings turned away from God and the religious ground-motive of apostasy took hold of their faith and of their whole temporal life.[13]

Western civilization, in its relentless rejection of divine revelation, finds itself in a Don Quixotic state—

tilting at windmills of its own making, ensnared in the delusions of self-determination. While it strives endlessly for freedom, it only tightens the chains of its own enslavement. Much like Don Quixote, the natural man does not fight against genuine injustices, but against the very fabric of reality itself. He seeks to redefine the creational order—what is good and evil, real and illusory, true and false—according to his own whims and desires. In his delusion, he perceives himself as a liberator; yet, in truth, he remains a captive to the very deceptions that he has himself devised.

As Harold Bloom astutely observes, "Don Quixote says that his quest is to destroy injustice. The final injustice is death, the ultimate bondage."[14] However, the question arises: what is the nature of the injustice Don Quixote seeks to destroy, if not his own self-imposed definition of it? And what, indeed, can this greatest injustice be, if not the unavoidable reality of his own mortality—principally, his ultimate subjugation as a created creature to the law of God? This, it seems, mirrors the very cry of modern man. He perceives every consequence of his sin as an affront to his supposed autonomy, viewing divine judgment not as righteous justice but as cosmic oppression. Yet, the ultimate tragedy lies in the fact that his rejection of God's law does not alter the objective reality of that law—it merely seals his eternal ruin.

The Folly of Western Thought

Herein lies the profound folly of the Freedom-Nature ground motive that underpins contemporary Western culture. The autonomous man wages war against the very structure of creation, convinced that his rebellion is a noble cause, yet he is blatantly blind to the truth that he is ultimately fighting against the immutable order of God—a *self-imposed* blindness, much like Don Quixote. Man elevates autonomy as his highest ideal, but this assertion of self-sufficiency ultimately leads only to his own destruction. He clings to unbelief, resisting every call to repentance, until death overtakes him. And in that final moment, as Bloom poignantly observes, "When he ceases to assert his autonomy, there is nothing left... no action remaining except to die."[15]

Yet, in stark contrast to the tragic futility of Don Quixote, there is genuine hope for those who have been awakened from their madness, for those now seeking to turn back to the truth. The solution to Western civilization's deepening malaise is not found in further self-invention or an unchecked pursuit of autonomy, but in the humble submission to the biblical framework of Creation-Fall-Redemption. In Christ alone, man discovers true freedom—not the illusory autonomy he so desperately seeks, but the freedom that comes from living in harmony with the law of God. This freedom is not a freedom to create one's own reality, but a freedom rooted in the divine law that governs all of creation. Only by yielding to Christ's Lordship does man cease his futile efforts to tilt at windmills, and in doing so, he finds peace in the eternal, unchanging reality that has always been.

Endnotes

1. Harold Bloom, "Introduction" in *Don Quixote: A New Translation by Edit Grossman* (New York, NY.: HarperCollins Pub., 2003), xxiii.

2. Vladimir Nabokov, *Lectures on Don Quixote*, ed. Fredson Bowers (New York, NY.: Harcourt Brace Jovanovich, 1983), 13, 20.

3. Alia E. Dastagir, "Marsha Blackburn asked Ketanji Brown Jackson to define 'woman.' Science says there's no simple answer", *USA Today*. Accessed October 8, 2023, https://www.usatoday.com/story/life/health-wellness/2022/03/24/marsha-blackburn-asked-ketanji-jackson-define-woman-science/7152439001/.

4. Bloom, "Introduction" in *Don Quixote*, xxv.

5. Nabokov, *Lectures on Dox Quixote*, 126-127.

6. Ibid, 126.

7. Ibid, 126.

8. Ibid., 127.

9. Miguel de Cervantes, *Don Quixote: A New Translation by Edit Grossman* (New York, NY.: HarperCollins Pub., 2003), 24.

10. Bloom, "Introduction" in *Don Quixote*, xxiii.

11. Herman Dooyeweerd, *The Roots of Western Culture*, (Jordan Station, ON.: Paideia Press, 2012), 20. Italicism mine.

12. Ibid., 117.

13. Ibid., 92.

14. Bloom, "Introduction" in *Don Quixote*, xxii.

15. Ibid., xxiii.

El Síndrome de Don Quijote

por Steven R. Martins

Un psiquiatra y su paciente

ERA UNA NOCHE tormentosa cuando un paciente entró en el consultorio de su psiquiatra. El viento aullaba afuera, y el golpeteo rítmico de la lluvia contra la ventana llenaba la habitación tenuemente iluminada. Tomó asiento en la silla reclinada, exhaló profundamente y fijó la vista en el techo.

—Me alegra verlo de nuevo, doctor —dijo—. Debo decir que la aflicción persiste. Quizá usted pueda ayudarme.

El psiquiatra, ya acomodado en su silla giratoria, con su bloc de notas abierto y la pluma en mano, respondió con la calma ensayada de quien ya lo ha escuchado todo antes.

—¿Y cuál es esa aflicción que lo aqueja?

—La misma de siempre, doctor. Veo lo que nadie más ve. Siento como si yo fuera el lunático.

—¿Y acaso eso no es precisamente su aflicción? —preguntó el psiquiatra retóricamente, levantando apenas la vista de sus notas—. Ya hemos hablado de esto en su última visita. Pero ya que está aquí, ¿por qué no me cuenta otra vez qué cree usted que lo aqueja?

—¡Pues claro, me aqueja la locura de los demás! —declaró el paciente.

El psiquiatra se recostó en su silla.

—¿Y cómo es eso?

El paciente se movió inquieto en su asiento, mirando por la ventana al otro lado del cuarto.

—Tome por ejemplo a su secretaria. ¿Sabe lo que me dijo al llegar?

—No lo sé —dijo el psiquiatra, levantando la mirada—. ¿Qué le dijo?

—Me dijo: "Está lloviendo a cántaros allá afuera".

—¿Y acaso no está lloviendo a cántaros?

—¡Claro que no! —El paciente hizo un gesto hacia la ventana—. El sol brilla espléndidamente. El cielo está despejado, como no podría estarlo más.

El psiquiatra lo observó cuidadosamente, sin siquiera mirar la ventana donde escuchaba la lluvia golpear.

—¿Y las gotas de agua en su chaqueta?

—Debo haber estado sudando profusamente.

—¿Las suelas mojadas de sus zapatos?

—Algún perro debió haberse aliviado junto a la entrada.

—¿Y el sonido del trueno retumbando a lo lejos?

—¿Ah, eso? —El paciente sonrió de lado—. ¿Se refiere a las interminables obras en las calles?

El psiquiatra suspiró, anotando algo en su cuaderno.

—Realmente no le importa lo que yo tenga que decir, ¿verdad? —preguntó el paciente.

El psiquiatra dejó la pluma a un lado.

—Permítame preguntarle esto: ¿por qué cree usted que ve las cosas tan diferente al resto del mundo, incluso cuando la realidad lo mira de frente?

El paciente soltó una risita ante la evidente observación, pensó un momento y luego respondió.

—Así que usted cree que el problema lo tengo yo. Pero dígame, doctor: si el mundo está loco, ¿no sigue de eso que el hombre cuerdo parecerá loco a sus ojos?

El psiquiatra lo estudió en silencio.

El paciente se puso de pie, se acomodó la chaqueta y caminó hacia la puerta. Antes de salir, miró hacia atrás.

—Gracias, doc. Usted debería hacerse revisar también. Está tan chiflado como todos los demás.

Cuando la puerta se cerró con un clic, el psiquiatra comenzó a golpear suavemente su bloc de notas con la pluma, absorto en sus pensamientos. Su mirada se desvió hacia la estantería a su lado, deteniéndose en un título familiar: *Don Quijote*. Una sonrisa astuta se dibujó en sus labios.

—Ah —murmuró—. Ya sé cómo voy a llamar a esto.

Pasó la página a una hoja limpia y, con letras mayúsculas bien marcadas, escribió:

SÍNDROME DE DON QUIJOTE

Rodeó las palabras con un bolígrafo rojo.

—Así es como lo llamaré —murmuró.

Luego, con una leve sonrisa burlona, añadió:

—Más vale que no se imagine que puede deshacerse de la factura que le espera.

Don Quijote como alegoría del hombre autónomo

La obra de ficción anterior ilustra la condición del hombre autónomo: espiritualmente ciego y atrapado en el autoengaño, incapaz de percibir la verdad incluso cuando la realidad se le presenta de frente. En este sentido, guarda una sorprendente semejanza con Don Quijote: ambos ven el mundo no como es, sino *como lo imaginan.*

Don Quijote, junto a su escudero Sancho Panza, es ampliamente reconocido como uno de los grandes personajes literarios de la literatura occidental, un clásico para todos los que hablan la lengua de Miguel de Cervantes. Sin embargo, más allá de su apariencia cómica, *Don Quijote* es una profunda alegoría del hombre caído en el mundo de Dios. Aunque no

sepamos si Cervantes lo pretendía, su obra sirve como una representación notable del hombre autónomo: aquel que, rechazando la verdad de la revelación divina, construye una realidad ilusoria en desafío al orden creado. Harold Bloom observó acertadamente que *Don Quijote* es, en su esencia, más una tragedia que una comedia. ¿Y qué es la historia del hombre pecador sino la mayor tragedia de todas?[1]

El estudioso literario ruso Vladimir Nabokov, en sus conferencias póstumas sobre *Don Quijote,* describe al protagonista antes de su autoimpuesta transformación:

Antes de nombrarse Don Quijote, su nombre es simplemente Quijada, o Quesada. Es un hidalgo de campo, propietario de un viñedo, una casa señorial y dos acres de tierra cultivable; un buen católico (que más tarde desarrollará una mala conciencia); un caballero alto, flaco, de unos cincuenta años... [Y] el hombre Sancho Panza. ¿Quién es él? Un labrador que había sido pastor en su juventud y, en algún momento, alguacil de una cofradía. Es un hombre de familia, pero vagabundo de corazón....[2]

Quijote y Sancho no son presentados como figuras fantásticas o surrealistas, sino como hombres co-

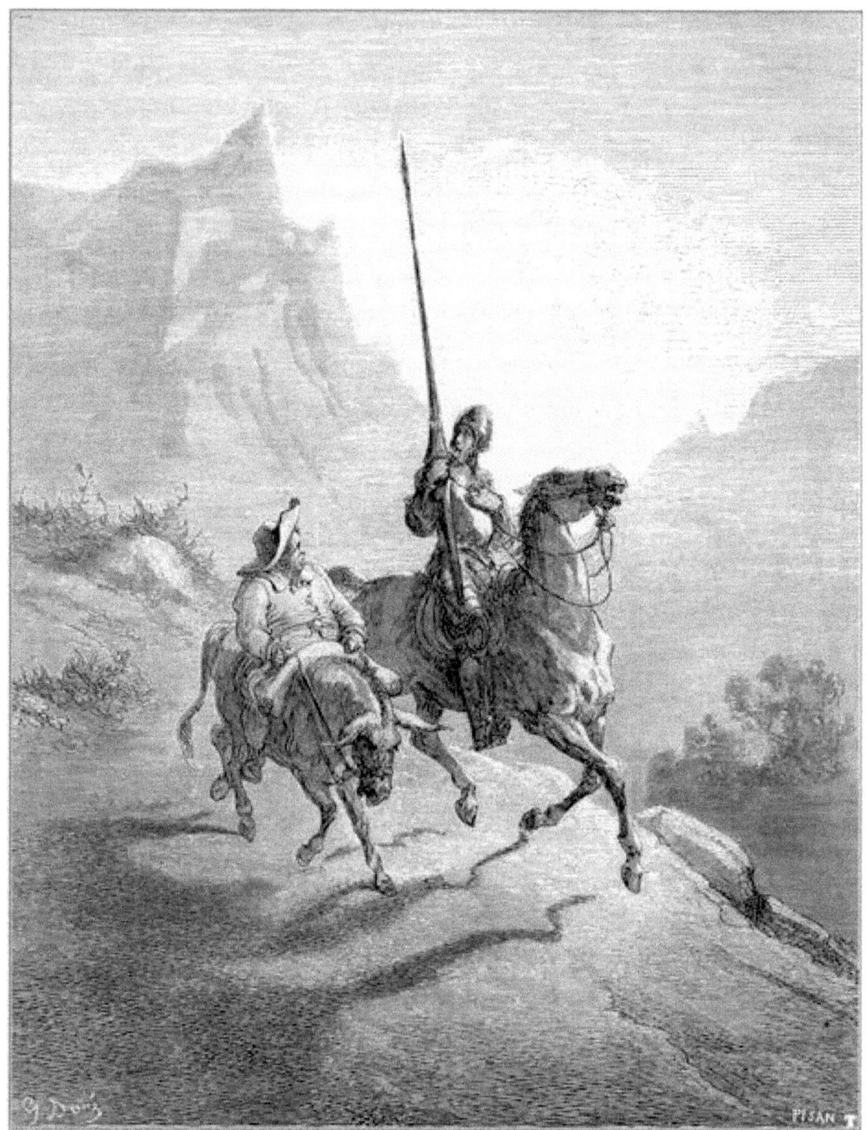

"Don Quijote y Sancho partiendo" (1863) de Gustave Doré.

munes y corrientes. Y, sin embargo, a medida que avanza la historia, son afligidos por una locura peculiar, percibiendo la realidad a través de un marco completamente desconectado de lo que realmente es. Este despren-dimiento de la realidad es la marca del hombre autónomo. Vive y respira en el mundo de Dios, conoce la verdad de todas las cosas en lo más profundo de su ser (Rom. 1:18), pero en su co-razón pecaminoso reprime esa verdad, construyendo en su lugar una ilusión que no concuerda en absoluto con la realidad.

Esta trágica *ilusión* es evidente en el mundo actual, donde el hombre autónomo —creyéndose independiente de Dios en todo sentido, y por tanto su propia autoridad suprema— rechaza la revelación divina para intentar redefinir incluso los aspectos más fundamentales de la realidad. Considérese, por ejemplo, un caso sorprendentemente moderno de esta rebelión: durante la audiencia de confirmación en EE. UU. de la jueza Ketanji Brown Jackson, la senadora Marsha Blackburn le planteó una pregunta sencilla: "¿Puede proporcionar una definición de la palabra 'mujer'?" Uno podría esperar una respuesta inmediata y evidente. Sin embargo, la respuesta de Jackson —"¿Puedo dar una definición? No puedo. No en este contexto, no soy bióloga."— no fue, en realidad, una respuesta. Quizá pueda parecer un momento risible, pero esto no es una comedia: es una tragedia.[3]

Podríamos preguntarnos: "¿Cree realmente el hombre pecador en sus propias ilusiones?" A la luz del caso citado, ¿*creía* sinceramente la jueza Jackson que su negativa a definir la palabra *mujer* —bajo el argumento de que no

tenía respuesta— estaba fundamentada en la verdad? En la superficie, parecería que sí. Después de todo, es la confesión del apóstata moderno. Pero en lo profundo del corazón humano, el hombre sabe que la ilusión es una mentira. El falso mundo del hombre no es más que un constructo artificial, una fachada erigida sobre la realidad, una que debe sostener constantemente para evitar que el peso aplastante de la verdad lo derrumbe. O, para decirlo en términos más bíblicos, debe *suprimir* incansablemente la verdad (Rom. 1:18), forzándola hacia abajo como quien empuja una pelota de playa bajo el agua, no sea que salga a la superficie y rompa su delirio.

Esta es precisamente la condición de Don Quijote. Vive por una ilusión, fabricando un mundo en el que él es un noble caballero andante, donde la realidad se dobla para ajustarse a su grandeza imaginada. Que nadie ose sugerir que no es caballero, y que nadie cuestione sus ilusiones —pues no solo deben ser toleradas, sino afirmadas como realidades verdaderas. Sin embargo, en lo profundo, él no cree del todo en la realidad de su propia visión. Bloom observa:

¿Cree Don Quijote por completo en la realidad de su propia visión? Evidentemente no, especialmente cuando él (y Sancho) es entregado por Cervantes a las bromas sadomasoquistas —de hecho, a las crueldades viciosas y humillantes— que afligen al caballero y a su escudero en la segunda parte.[4]

Un ejemplo particularmente vívido de esta tensión entre ilusión y realidad se encuentra en el capítulo 18 de *Don Quijote*. Nabokov resume la escena en la que Quijote, atrapado por una "extraña locura," confunde dos rebaños de ovejas, junto con el polvo que levantan, con dos poderosos ejércitos. En esta escena, Sancho protesta:

> —Señor, —dijo Sancho— ¡que yo me vaya al diablo si veo un solo hombre, gigante o caballero de todos esos de quienes vuestra merced habla! ¿Quién sabe? Quizá sea otro encantamiento, como el de anoche.[5]

Don Quijote, sin embargo, no quiere oír nada de eso:

> —¿Cómo puedes decir eso? —replicó Don Quijote—. ¿Acaso no oyes el relinchar de los caballos, el sonido de las trompetas, el redoble de los tambores?[6]

A lo que Sancho responde, desconcertado:

> —No oigo nada —dijo Sancho—, excepto el balido de las ovejas.[7]

Uno esperaría que Don Quijote despertara a lo absurdo de su ilusión al cabalgar entre el rebaño de ovejas. Seguramente, con una evidencia tan abrumadora en contra de su creencia, admitiría su locura. Pero no —en cambio, se aferra aún más, culpando a un mago siniestro por su desgracia:

> —Esto, —dijo Don Quijote—, es obra de ese ladrón de mago, mi enemigo, que así falsea las cosas y las hace desaparecer. Has de saber, Sancho, que para ellos es muy fácil hacernos asumir cualquier apariencia que elijan; y así, ese maligno que me persigue, envidioso de la gloria que vio que estaba a punto de alcanzar en esta batalla, convirtió los escuadrones del enemigo en rebaños de ovejas.[8]

Esta es la condición del hombre autónomo. Cada día se enfrenta a la verdad —por dondequiera que mire, la realidad testifica en su contra. Sin embargo, no puede ceder. Debe persistir en su engaño, sin importar cuán abrumadora sea la evidencia en su contra.[9] Y en verdad, solo hay una forma verdadera de evidencia: *la evidencia de Dios*; porque cualquier cosa que el hombre autónomo afirme en su defensa no es más que una interpretación distorsionada de lo que Dios ha revelado en Su orden creado. Para el hombre autónomo, la irracionalidad del pecado prevalece sobre cualquier apelación a la *razón*, pues sus propias facultades están esclavizadas a su rebelión. Y aquí radica la futilidad de intentar razonar al pecador hacia la fe salvadora aparte de la obra del Espíritu de Dios. ¿Acaso no tiene, como Don Quijote, momentos en los que vacila, en los que percibe que algo anda terriblemente mal con su ilusión? Ciertamente. Pero esos momentos son fugaces, y su locura —su *necedad*, como la llama la Escritura (Sal. 14:1; Rom. 1:22)— es más fuerte que todo lo demás. Mientras permanezca autónomo, es decir, en abierta rebelión contra Dios y Su ley, sus facultades no servirán a la verdad, sino que estarán atadas a la supresión de ella.

Así, no estamos tratando meramente con un error intelectual, sino con la profunda esclavitud espiritual del pecado que aflige al hombre autónomo. Se requiere nada menos que la gracia soberana de Dios para romper la ilusión del pecador, despojándolo de las falsedades a las que tan desesperadamente se aferra. Solo mediante la obra eficaz del Espíritu puede la mente del hombre ser renovada, y solo a través del testimonio de la Palabra viva

de Dios puede su corazón ser vuelto de las tinieblas a la luz. Hasta entonces, el hombre, atado a su síndrome quijotesco, seguirá lanzándose contra molinos de viento, convencido de que son gigantes. Persistirá en llamar ejército a un rebaño, sordo al sonido de su balido. En resumen, redefinirá la misma realidad para ajustarla a su narrativa autoimpuesta, para su propia perdición, incluso mientras toda la creación testifica en su contra. Y al final, como Don Quijote, descubrirá que cuando su ilusión finalmente se derrumbe, no quedará nada —ninguna acción restante, salvo morir,[10] si elige no arrepentirse y rendirse a Dios.

El desarrollo del pensamiento occidental

Sería difícil argumentar que el síndrome "quijotesco" del hombre surgió en un vacío, como si hubiera aparecido "espontáneamente" sin explicación racional ni causalidad lógica. Más bien, el síndrome quijotesco debe entenderse dentro de un contexto mucho más amplio.

Ante todo, este síndrome quijotesco es consecuencia del pecado de nuestros primeros padres. Su transgresión original —la búsqueda de una autonomía radical, el deseo de existir independientemente de Dios en todo sentido y convertirse en dioses— trajo no solo la caída del mundo (Gén. 3:17-19), evidente en las realidades omnipresentes de injusticia, sufrimiento, muerte y decadencia, sino también la corrupción de la orientación fundamental de la vida humana, especialmente en el ámbito del pensamiento (Jer. 17:9; Rom. 1:21-22; Ef. 4:17-18).

Dada esta distorsión intelectual, es prudente examinar el desarrollo histórico del pensamiento de la civilización occidental. En pocas palabras, el estado actual del hombre caído —es decir, estar afligido por el síndrome quijotesco— no carece de precedentes, sino que es más bien la culminación de siglos de desarrollo filosófico y teológico arraigado en presuposiciones falsas y antitéticas.

¿Cómo abarcar una extensión tan vasta de tiempo mientras encapsulamos con precisión el desarrollo histórico del pensamiento occidental? Para empezar, debemos reconocer que la historia intelectual de Occidente está moldeada por cosmovisiones distintas —una cosmovisión es una red de presuposiciones que se originan en el corazón. En este sentido, también podríamos decir que la historia intelectual de Occidente está moldeada por compromisos fundamentales del corazón que influyen en el pensamiento del hombre y, en consecuencia, en la sociedad en la que vive. Como observa el difunto filósofo cristiano neerlandés Herman Dooyeweerd (1894–1977) en su obra seminal *Las raíces de la cultura occidental*, estas cosmovisiones pueden clasificarse en cuatro motivos-raíz fundamentales. Tres de ellos son apóstatas tanto en su estructura (sus presuposiciones) como en su dirección (aquello que se adora), mientras que solo uno es fiel en su estructura (es decir, corresponde a la realidad) y en su dirección (orientado a la adoración del único Dios verdadero). Estos motivos-raíz son: (i) el esquema Materia-Forma de la filosofía griega, (ii) el esquema Gracia-Naturaleza del escolasticismo medieval, (iii) la dicotomía Libertad-Naturaleza de la Ilustración, y (iv) el marco Creación-Caída-Redención de la Reforma —el único de los cuatro motivos-raíz que *no* es apóstata. Históricamente, el marco Creación-Caída-Redención de la Reforma sigue al del escolasticismo medieval, pero para distinguirlo claramente de los motivos-raíz apóstatas, lo he colocado al final. En el contexto del pensamiento contemporáneo, la dicotomía Libertad-Naturaleza es la más pertinente; sin embargo, antes de proceder, una comprensión adecuada requiere trazar la progresión ideológica que condujo primero a ella.

El esquema Materia-Forma del pensamiento griego

No se puede negar que la antigua civilización griega desempeñó un papel formativo en la configuración de la tradición intelectual occidental. Entre sus pensadores más influyentes se encuentran Platón y Aristóteles, cuyo dualismo Materia-Forma postulaba dos reinos distintos e irreconciliables: el mundo de la *Materia*, en el que vivimos, y el mundo de las *Formas*, que existe más allá de lo material. En términos generales, esta tradición intelectual consideraba el mundo material como nada más que una mera sombra de una realidad superior e inmutable. Por ejemplo, un caballo en el mundo material era entendido como una representación imperfecta de una "caballosidad" idealizada que existía en el reino de las *Formas*. Lo mismo podía decirse de la belleza: se entendía como una representación imperfecta de una "bellezosidad" idealizada que existía en el reino de las *Formas*. ¿Y cómo llegaba el hombre, supuestamente, a conocer estas *Formas*? Según la doctrina de la *anamnesis* (reminiscencia) de Platón, el alma del hombre —antes

de quedar confinada dentro del cuerpo material— provenía del propio reino de las *Formas*. El hombre no aprende algo nuevo, simplemente recuerda memorias perdidas de antes de su encarnación. Este dualismo Materia-Forma impregnó la cultura griega, como explica Dooyeweerd:

> El motivo griego de la *materia*, el principio informe de devenir y decadencia, estaba orientado al aspecto del movimiento en la realidad temporal. Este motivo dio al pensamiento griego y a toda la cultura griega un matiz de misterio oscuro que es ajeno al pensamiento moderno. El motivo griego de la forma, por otro lado, estaba orientado al aspecto cultural de la realidad temporal ("cultura" significa esencialmente la formación libre de la materia). Este motivo dirigía constantemente el pensamiento hacia una *forma* de ser extrasensorial e imperecedera que trascendía el flujo cíclico de la vida.[11]

Esta fragmentación de la realidad, sin embargo, no es meramente un error intelectual, sino una consecuencia directa de la condición caída del hombre. La Caída (Rom. 1:18–25), además de introducir la maldición del pecado y la muerte en el mundo, corrompió la capacidad de razón del hombre, resultando en una supresión de la verdad y una aceptación de percepciones distorsionadas de la realidad. La cosmovisión griega antigua ejemplificó esta supresión en su marco filosófico: una manifestación temprana de la mala interpretación de la creación por parte de la humanidad, una que no logró reconocer la unidad y coherencia del orden de Dios.

El esquema Gracia-Naturaleza del escolasticismo

Lo que siguió a los griegos fue un profundo encuentro entre la revelación bíblica y el pensamiento griego, poco después del surgimiento del cristianismo. A medida que la iglesia primitiva (particularmente los padres de la iglesia) lidiaba con preguntas de teología y filosofía, las categorías griegas fueron moldeando cada vez más su marco intelectual. Este encuentro culminó en la tradición escolástica medieval, desarrollada plenamente por Tomás de Aquino, que introdujo el esquema Gracia-Naturaleza. Dentro de este marco, la realidad se dividía en dos reinos distintos: *Gracia*, que representaba todo lo sagrado, y *Naturaleza*, que abarcaba el mundo caído, incluida la filosofía griega. El escolasticismo sostenía que la *Gracia* perfeccionaba la *Naturaleza*, aunque ambas seguían siendo fundamentalmente distintas.

Este dualismo planteaba un problema teológico inherente: ¿cómo podían reconciliarse lo divino y lo profano? Aunque el escolasticismo buscaba una síntesis, no lograba captar toda la profundidad de la depravación humana, tratando el pecado como una mera debilidad en lugar de una corrupción fundamental del corazón. Aristóteles y Platón, por más brillante que fuera su filosofía, eran paganos cuya razón estaba inevitablemente manchada por la Caída. Suponer que sus ideas podían armonizarse con la revelación divina *sin una distorsión consecuente* era subestimar los efectos radicales del pecado. Dooyeweerd critica este intento:

La visión griega de la naturaleza en Aristóteles era pagana. Sin embargo, el motivo-raíz de naturaleza y gracia del catolicismo romano buscó acomodar el motivo-raíz griego al de la revelación divina. Los escolásticos argumentaban que todo lo sujeto al nacimiento y la muerte, incluidos los seres humanos, estaba constituido de materia y forma. Dios había creado todas las cosas según este orden. Como ser *natural*, por ejemplo, sostenían que una persona consiste en un "alma racional" y un "cuerpo material." Caracterizada por su capacidad de pensar, el alma racional era tanto la "forma esencial e invisible" del cuerpo como una "sustancia" imperecedera que podía existir aparte del cuerpo... Pero esta "naturaleza" humana, que está guiada por la luz natural de la razón, no fue corrompida por el pecado y, por tanto, tampoco necesita ser restaurada por Cristo. La naturaleza humana solo fue "debilitada" por la caída. Continúa siendo fiel a su "ley natural" innata y posee una autonomía, una independencia y autodeterminación relativas en oposición al ámbito de la gracia de la religión cristiana.[12]

Aquí radica el defecto fundamental del escolasticismo: trató la razón natural como autónoma —es decir, como neutral e independiente—, minimizando así la corrupción total del pecado. Al afirmar que la razón estaba meramente debilitada y no completamente caída, el escolasticismo sentó las bases para una visión compartimentada de la realidad. Esto es más evidente en la división sagrado-secular que persiste en gran parte del pensamiento contemporáneo, donde ciertos aspectos de la vida se consideran "espirituales" y por lo tanto *privados*, mientras que otros se consideran "neutrales" o "seculares" y por lo tanto *públicos*. Tal dicotomía es incompatible con la soberanía de Dios y Su gobierno sobre todas las cosas.

El marco Creación-Caída-Redención de la Reforma

Lo que siguió históricamente fue el surgimiento de la Reforma protestante, que introdujo un nuevo motivo-raíz —el único de los cuatro que refleja fielmente la realidad. Lo que hizo la Reforma fue exponer las peligrosas implicaciones del dualismo escolástico, haciendo un llamado a volver a la autoridad absoluta de las Escrituras (*Sola Scriptura*). Los reformadores rechazaron la noción de que la razón humana pudiera funcionar de manera *autónoma* respecto a la revelación divina. En su lugar, articularon un marco bíblico integral: el motivo-raíz Creación-Caída-Redención. Este paradigma reconoce que:

1. **Creación**—Dios creó todas las cosas buenas, y el orden creado refleja Su estructura y propósito divinos.

2. **Caída**—El pecado ha corrompido no solo la naturaleza humana, sino todos los aspectos de la realidad, distorsionando relaciones, instituciones e incluso el mundo natural.

Redención—La obra redentora de Cristo se extiende más allá de la salvación individual hacia la restauración de todo el orden creado.

A diferencia de las cosmovisiones anteriores, este marco rechazó la validez del pensamiento dualista. No había dualismo Materia-Forma, ni dualismo Gracia-Naturaleza, y por lo tanto, tampoco una división sagrado-secular; toda la vida caía bajo el reino soberano de Cristo. Esto significaba que la filosofía, la política, la ciencia y las artes no debían operar sobre la base de un razonamiento humano autónomo, sino ser sometidas y reorientadas según la verdad bíblica.

Los reformadores, en esencia, entendieron que la Caída había corrompido todos los aspectos de la existencia humana, y que, por lo tanto, se necesitaba una redención integral. Así surgió el marco Creación-Caída-Redención como la comprensión de la realidad por parte del hombre a la luz de la Palabra de Dios. Pero mientras figuras como Juan Calvino y Martín Lutero buscaron purgar el pensamiento cristiano de sus enredos escolásticos, muchos de sus seguidores, sin darse cuenta, los reintrodujeron por la puerta trasera. En consecuencia, aunque las implicaciones de este motivo-raíz fueron genuinamente transformadoras —dando forma, o mejor dicho, *reformando*, de manera fundamental la trayectoria del pensamiento occidental—, permaneció susceptible al compromiso intelectual. Esta concesión lo dejó vulnerable al movimiento de contrarrespuesta que pronto surgiría, uno que buscaba rechazar por completo la autoridad divina.

La dicotomía Libertad-Naturaleza de la Ilustración

La Ilustración, surgida como reacción contra la Reforma, buscó reafirmar la autonomía humana estableciendo un nuevo motivo-raíz: el esquema Libertad-Naturaleza. Esta cosmovisión postulaba una tensión irreconciliable entre las leyes deterministas de la *Naturaleza* y el ideal de la *Libertad* humana. Los pensadores ilustrados imaginaban el mundo (*Naturaleza*) como un vasto sistema mecanicista gobernado por leyes inmutables, mientras que al mismo tiempo insistían en la capacidad del hombre para trascender esas restricciones mediante la razón y la autodeterminación (*Libertad*).

Sin embargo, esta dicotomía resultó ser inherentemente contradictoria. Si la *Naturaleza* está gobernada por leyes fijas, ¿cómo puede el hombre

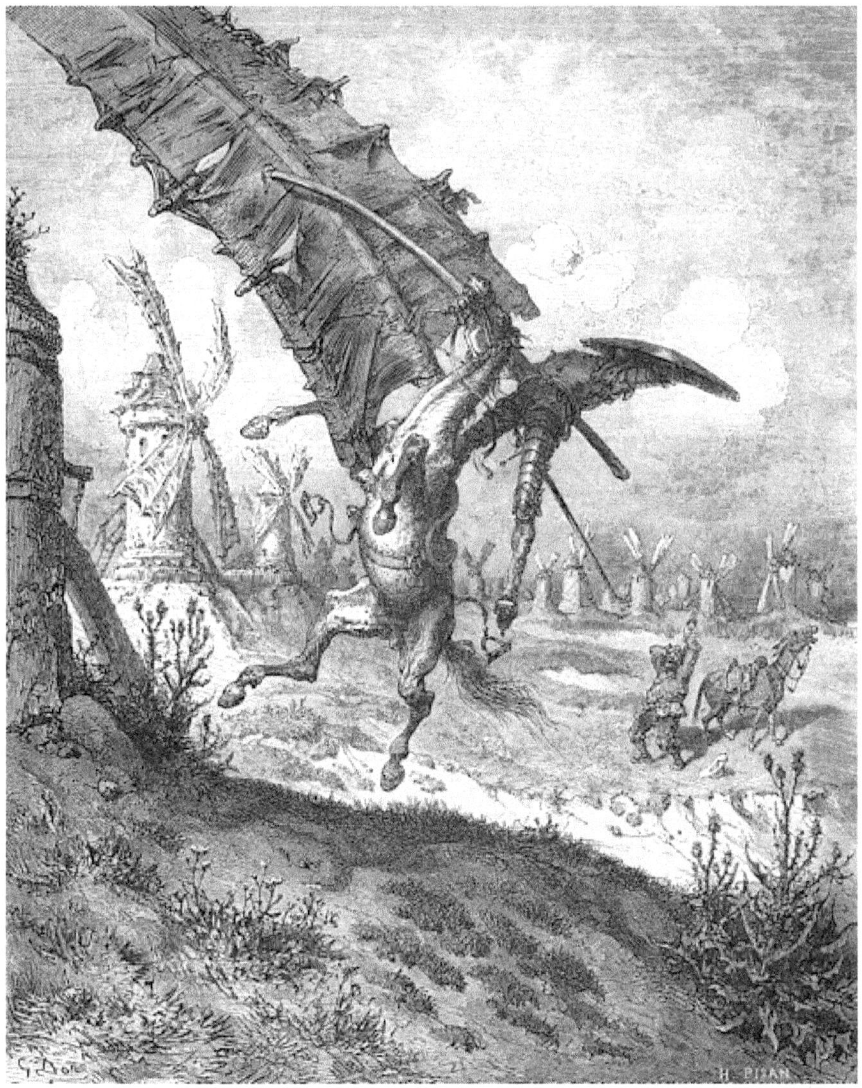

"Don Quijote y el molino de viento" (1863) de Gustave Doré.

poseer verdadera *Libertad*? Si todo está determinado, ¿cómo puede existir la autonomía? Esta tensión no resuelta condujo a una crisis en el pensamiento occidental.

Si tuviéramos que identificar el motivo-raíz dominante de nuestra cultura actual, sin duda sería el esquema Libertad-Naturaleza, ahora moldeado más por el Romanticismo que por el Racionalismo. El fracaso del racionalismo ilustrado —su incapacidad para satisfacer los anhelos existenciales y espirituales de la humanidad— allanó el camino al Romanticismo, un movimiento que rechazó el frío empirismo en favor de la emoción y la imaginación. Aquí, la búsqueda de autonomía alcanzó su punto máximo: el hombre, liberado de las restricciones de la razón, buscó definir la realidad en sus propios términos. Las consecuencias son evidentes en el pensamiento moderno: el rechazo de la verdad objetiva, el auge del subjetivismo radical y el dominio del emocionalismo sobre el discurso racional. ¿Cómo explicar esto, sino diciendo que el famoso "Pienso, luego existo" de René Descartes ha dado paso al moderno *"Siento, luego existo"*?

Comprendiendo mejor el síndrome quijotesco

La historia intelectual de Occidente, en muchos aspectos, puede entenderse como la narrativa desplegada de la trágica rebelión de la humanidad contra Dios y Su orden creacional. Desde los dualismos inherentes a la filosofía griega, pasando por la síntesis intentada por el escolasticismo, hasta la afirmación radical de la autonomía humana en la Ilustración, cada etapa revela las consecuencias de un corazón apóstata. Como observó agudamente Dooyeweerd, el problema fundamental no es meramente una divergencia intelectual, sino de profunda importancia espiritual:

> Todo [ello] surge de la raíz religiosa de nuestra vida temporal, es decir, del corazón, alma o espíritu de la persona. A causa de la caída en pecado, los corazones de los seres humanos se apartaron de Dios, y el motivo-raíz religioso de la apostasía se apoderó de su fe y de toda su vida temporal.[13]

La civilización occidental, en su rechazo implacable de la revelación divina, se encuentra en un estado quijotesco —lanzándose contra molinos de viento creados por ella misma, atrapada en los delirios de la autodeterminación. Mientras se esfuerza sin cesar por alcanzar la libertad, no hace más que apretar las cadenas de su propia esclavitud. Al igual que Don Quijote, el hombre natural no lucha contra injusticias genuinas, sino contra el propio tejido de la realidad. Busca redefinir el orden creacional —lo que es bueno y malo, real e ilusorio, verdadero y falso— conforme a sus propios caprichos y deseos. En su delirio, se percibe a sí mismo como un libertador; pero, en verdad, permanece cautivo de los mismos engaños que él mismo ha ideado.

Como observa agudamente Harold Bloom: *"Don Quijote dice que su misión es destruir la injusticia. La injusticia final es la muerte, la esclavitud última."*[14] Sin embargo, surge la pregunta: ¿cuál es la naturaleza de la injusticia que Don Quijote busca destruir, si no es su propia definición autoimpuesta de ella? ¿Y cuál puede ser, en verdad, esta mayor injusticia, si no es la realidad inevitable de su propia mortalidad —principalmente, su sometimiento último como criatura creada a la ley de Dios? Esto, al parecer, refleja el mismo clamor del hombre moderno. Percibe cada consecuencia de su pecado como una afrenta a su supuesta autonomía, viendo el juicio divino no como justicia recta, sino como opresión cósmica. Sin embargo, la tragedia última radica en el hecho de que su rechazo de la ley de Dios no altera la realidad objetiva de esa ley —simplemente sella su ruina eterna.

La necedad del pensamiento occidental

Aquí radica la profunda necedad del motivo-raíz Libertad-Naturaleza que sustenta la cultura occidental contemporánea. El hombre autónomo libra una guerra contra la propia estructura de la creación, convencido de que su rebelión es una causa noble, y sin embargo, es descaradamente ciego a la verdad de que en última instancia está luchando contra el orden inmutable de Dios —una ceguera *autoimpuesta*, muy similar a la de Don Quijote. El hombre eleva la autonomía como su ideal supremo, pero esta afirmación de autosuficiencia finalmente lo conduce solo a su propia destrucción. Se aferra a la incredulidad, resistiendo cada llamado al arrepentimiento, hasta que la muerte lo alcanza. Y en ese momento final, como observa conmovedoramente Bloom, "Cuando deja de afirmar su autonomía, no queda nada... ninguna acción restante, salvo morir."[15]

Sin embargo, en marcado contraste con la trágica futilidad de Don Quijote, hay una esperanza genuina para aquellos que han despertado de su locura, para quienes ahora buscan volver a la verdad. La solución al creciente malestar de la civilización occidental no se encuentra en una mayor auto-invención ni en una búsqueda desenfrenada de autonomía, sino en la humilde sumisión al marco bíblico de Creación-Caída-Redención. Solo en Cristo el hombre descubre la verdadera libertad —no la autonomía ilusoria que tan desesperadamente busca, sino la libertad que proviene de vivir en armonía con la ley de Dios. Esta libertad no es una libertad para crear una realidad propia, sino una libertad arraigada en la ley divina que gobierna toda la creación. Solo al rendirse al señorío de Cristo el hombre cesa sus esfuerzos fútiles de lanzarse contra molinos de viento, y al hacerlo, encuentra paz en la realidad eterna e inmutable que siempre ha estado allí.

LA FUENTE: IBEROAMERICAN JOURNAL FOR CHRISTIAN WORLDVIEW

no es una libertad para crear una realidad propia, sino una libertad arraigada en la ley divina que gobierna toda la creación. Solo al rendirse al señorío de Cristo el hombre cesa sus esfuerzos fútiles de lanzarse contra molinos de viento, y al hacerlo, encuentra paz en la realidad eterna e inmutable que siempre ha estado allí.

Notas Finales

1   Harold Bloom, "Introduction" en *Don Quixote: A New Translation by Edit Grossman* (New York, NY.: HarperCollins Pub., 2003), xxiii.

2   Vladimir Nabokov, *Lectures on Don Quixote*, ed. Fredson Bowers (New York, NY.: Harcourt Brace Jovanovich, 1983), 13, 20.

3   Alia E. Dastagir, "Marsha Blackburn asked Ketanji Brown Jackson to define 'woman.' Science says there's no simple answer", *USA Today*. Consultado 8 de octubre, 2023, https://www.usatoday.com/story/life/health-wellness/2022/03/24/marsha-blackburn-asked-ketanji-jackson-define-woman-science/7152439001/.

4   Bloom, "Introduction" en *Don Quixote*, xxv.

5   Nabokov, *Lectures on Dox Quixote*, 126-127.

6   Ibid, 126.

7   Ibid, 126.

8   Ibid., 127.

9   Miguel de Cervantes, *Don Quixote: A New Translation by Edit Grossman* (New York, NY.: HarperCollins Pub., 2003), 24.

10   Bloom, "Introduction" en *Don Quixote*, xxiii.

11   Herman Dooyeweerd, *The Roots of Western Culture*, (Jordan Station, ON.: Paideia Press, 2012), 20. Italicism mine.

12   Ibid., 117.

13   Ibid., 92.

14   Bloom, "Introduction" in *Don Quixote*, xxii.

15   Ibid., xxiii.

Art and the Cultural Mandate

by Ryan Eras

IN MANY Christian circles it is common to talk about the Bible's 'cultural mandate.' This is first revealed in Genesis 1, when God tells Adam and Eve to "be fruitful and multiply; fill the earth and subdue it; have dominion over the fish of the sea, over the birds of the air, and over every living thing that moves on the earth" (Gen. 1:28). This mandate is reiterated and clarified in the Great Commission, when Christ tells His followers to make disciples of all nations. In brief, the cultural mandate is the charge to man as God's image-bearers to tend and keep the created world, faithfully developing it in ways that honour God and that bless others. It applies in all spheres of life, from thoughtful and knowledgeable decisions of what and how to farm a field, to faithful and godly deliberations about how to govern a country. When we exercise godly dominion, the Lord promises to pour out His blessing on our work and our world (Psalm 72:1-8).

In the following paragraphs, I want to take the overarching command of the cultural mandate, and the promises in God's holy and eternal Word that the whole earth will be filled with the glory of the Lord, and think about what these things mean for us in one particular cultural sphere, the area of art, and of human creativity.

Defining Terms—Art and Meaning

Without wishing to insult anyone's intelligence, let's first define our terms. For present purposes, by 'art' I mean the fine arts generally—visual art and related things like architecture and sculpture, as well as music, poetry, literature, dance, theater, and more recently, filmmaking. This is to distinguish the fine arts from the liberal arts. The liberal arts are so called because by pursuing them, they are the arts that help make us *free*—arts like history, literature, theology, and philosophy—by helping us understand and interact with the world. 'Fine' arts simply means the finished arts, they are what we make as free people. In short, the primary purpose of the fine arts is not to be useful for some other end; it is art for its own sake.

Still, resting underneath all of that, the question remains, what is art? Books have been written, and careers have been built around this question, but the Christian philosopher Calvin Seerveld cuts through much of the ideological noise when he says that,

> Art is a much less baffling matter than it is often made out to be. To me art means style. Art is the symbolical objectification of certain meaning aspects of a thing subject to the law of allusivity.[1]

This is a somewhat technical way of saying that art is something man makes which shows, rather than tells, its message. And it is acknowledged as 'art' to the extent that it express-es something true and meaningful about the world. This should not be controversial, but as Western society began abandoning its obedience to God and His Word, we also lost the understanding and consensus on what qualifies as art. Andrew Kern explains: "Prior to the Enlightenment, Europeans at least, and I think most cultures, used art to embody meanings that they believed themselves to have identified in the world as it is." So if we are to create or evaluate art from a distinctly Christian perspective, our critique will center around whether a work of art brings glory to God.

Spirit-filled Creativity

God cares about beauty – creation didn't merely function, it was "very good." In her book *The Mind of the Maker*, the educator and scholar Dorothy L. Sayers starts by considering the question "what is man?" and she starts at the Bible's account of the creation of man. We know from this account that man is created in the image of God, and Sayers writes that while we have man, the image-bearer, in front of us, at this point in the biblical narrative, we are not told much about what God is like. If we bear the image of God, what exactly is the *content* of that image? Sayers observes that the one thing we know at this point in world history is that God creates, and that what He creates is good.[2]

The Westminster Shorter Catechism teaches that the chief end of man is to glorify God and enjoy Him forever. One of the Scripture proofs for this claim is Ephesians 2:10, where Paul explains to the Ephesian Christians that we are God's workmanship. As works of art ourselves, we are to make other works of art, and both we and our works are meant to glorify. Bringing glory to God should be the Christian's criterion for determining whether something is good art, bad art, or not art. The universe is full of meaning, because creation is fully dependent on the Word of God who spoke it into being, and who sustains it at every moment. The meaning of creation is to point back to, and give glory to, the Creator. This is true of the things He creates, and also of the things we, as His image-bearers, create.

Another reason we need art is that we cannot go against our God-given nature. Creativity is rooted in what it means to be human, and in God's dealings with His people, this creative nature is prominently on display. Consider this detail in the Lord's instructions to Moses for building the tabernacle in Exodus 31:

> [1] Now the Lord spoke to Moses, saying, [2] "See, I have called by name Bezalel, the son of Uri, the son of Hur, of the tribe of Judah. [3] I have filled him with the Spirit of God in wisdom, in understanding, in knowledge, and in all kinds of craftsmanship, [4] to make artistic designs for work in gold, in silver, and in bronze, [5] and in the cutting of stones for settings, and in the carving of wood, that he may work in all kinds of craftsmanship. [6] And behold, I Myself have appointed with him Oholiab, the son of Ahisamach, of the tribe of Dan; and in the hearts of all who are skillful I have put skill, that they may make all that I have commanded you.

Don't miss this: Bezalel and Oholiab were filled with the Spirit of God—this was a very rare event in the Old Testament, and God did it for these artisans, because beauty matters to God. It is one of the principal ways that we bring God glory.

Of course, not everyone is called to be a professional artist. But the aesthetic aspect is inalienable to what it means to be human; we can't help but create, and we can't help but have an aesthetic sensibility. If you've ever chosen paint colours or furniture for your house, or shoes for your feet, you made aesthetic choices.

Retreat to Commitment

When Christians hear about the contemporary sphere of art, however, we don't generally think of it as a particularly godly area of culture. Most of us think of outrageous, random conceptual pieces that nobody understands, that claim to be making a deep statement about some aspect of life, but most of the time are just meant to shock or confuse. And this is only what we should expect, because an artist who doesn't believe that there is order and meaning to life will reflect that belief in their art. This is how we get purported art exhibits consisting of broken chunks of concrete on a plate, and some guy in purple glasses telling us it's a symbol of suburban alienation.

If you have ever visited, and especially if you have ever brought a group of young people through an exhibit like this, you will hear a repeated comment muttered at each display: "I could do that." This comment is a recognition of the key problem with what's called conceptual art: the only power it has is in the concept. The English philosopher Roger Scruton, in his documentary film *Why Beau-*

ty Matters, illustrates this point well when he says:

> You just need to say, 'half a cow, floating in a tank of formaldehyde'—and you're there. The only skill involved in that piece is coming from the butcher who gives you the half cow. You don't accomplish anything further by actually carrying out the concept in real life.[3]

Because God designed us to recognize and appreciate true beauty, we rightly respond to such displays with dismissiveness or contempt. This is a natural response, but in our rejection of such *anti*-art, we must take care not to abandon the entire sphere of art.

'Christian Art'

Unhappily, this is exactly what has happened in much of Western Christianity. I believe that Christians have faithlessly abandoned a key part of our rightful, God-given inheritance as His image-bearers by allowing the enemies of God to control the arts. Christians have a right and a responsibility to make good art, and the sad reality is that we've often forfeited that; we have neglected our duty to the cultural mandate.

Instead of making better art, that glorifies God, and that says something true about the world, we've retreated to Christian ghettoes where we can use our Christian clichés and where no unbelievers bother about us. Instead of just trying to make great music, we listen to the most popular secular bands, and then try to assemble a copycat Christian version. We make Christian films with lame stories that follow a predictable and totally unrealistic conversion narrative.

Andrew Kern describes the current Christian film scene:

> Movies made by Christians for the Christian world tend to present the world as a place where just people end up getting things their way in the end. They endure trials and then end up victorious. However, I can't help but wonder if it isn't misleading and maybe failing to prepare for reality. Sometimes reality is utterly crushing. Utterly, unbearably crushing. And it doesn't get made right... Christianity does not advocate for the Hallmark channel...for the sappy, overly charming, emotionally uplifting kitsch.

We've let the enemies of God build and then monopolize all the biggest media platforms, and we've surrendered without a fight. This is what Douglas Wilson calls a retreat to commitment. We surrender the field where the real cultural battles are being fought, and huddle together in a Christian ghetto, and we say we're making a stand. We act like we're being faithful because we make films with scripts that talk about prayer and about God, and overcoming hardships, and doing all things through Christ, but what many of these films are actually doing is faithless. The reason much contemporary Christian art is bad art is because it lies about God by not presenting the world in a truthful way, refusing to acknowledge that real life is messy and dangerous and sometimes not at all to our tastes.

The God Who Speaks

As Christians, we worship a creative, creating, speaking God. All the other gods are worthless idols. The only reason anyone is creative is because God has given us creativity. For this reason, Christians need to reject the cowardly lie that unbelieving art, music and film is the standard; we need to stop assuming that the world is better at this, and stop taking our cues from the world in our own creative output. We need to remember that we bear the image of our Maker, and that we have the Holy Spirit, Who guides us in all truth, and we need to make are that reflects this reality.

Endnotes

1   Calvin Seerveld, "A Look at Books," *The Outlook Magazine*, 1963, p. 39.

2   Dorothy L. Sayers, *The Mind of the Maker,* London: Methuen, 1941, p. 3.

3   Roger Scruton. *Why Beauty Matters*. Directed by Paul G. Allen. 2009. London: BBC, 2009.

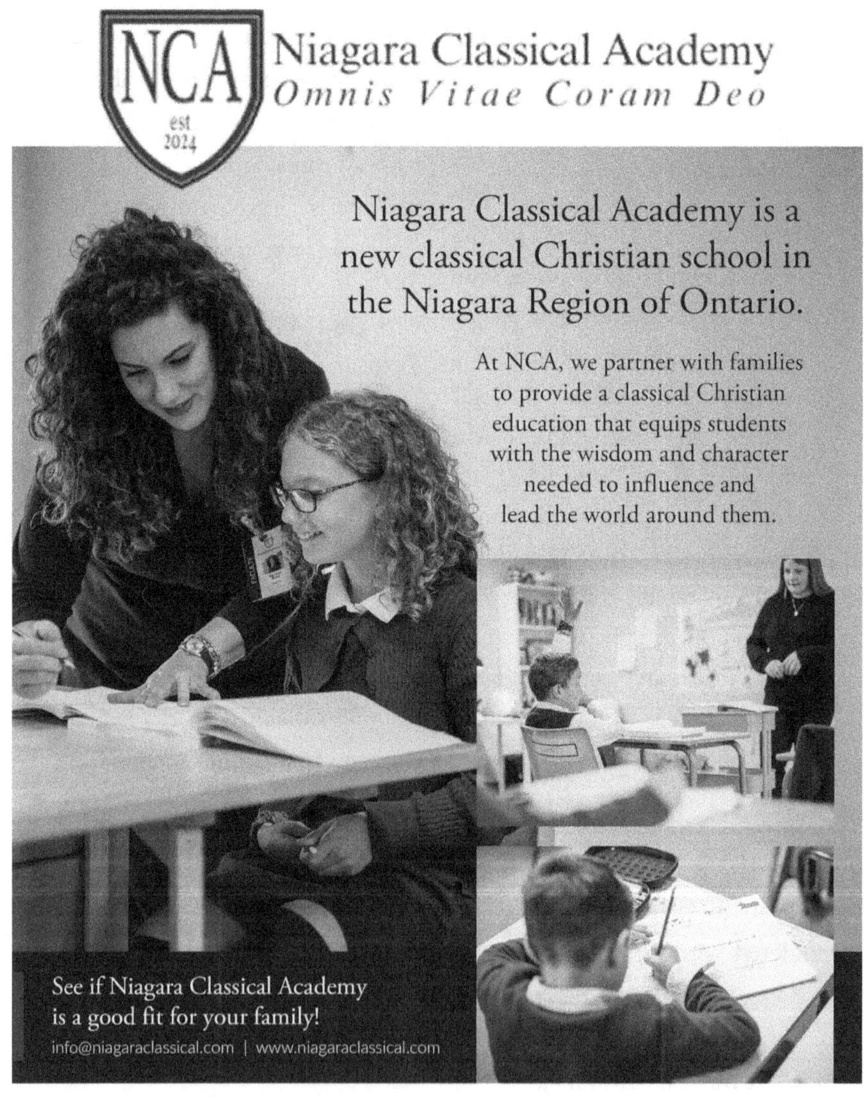

Arte y el Mandato Cultural

por Ryan Eras

Arte y el Mandato Cultural

EN MUCHOS círculos cristianos es común hablar del "mandato cultural" de la Biblia. Esto se revela por primera vez en Génesis 1, cuando Dios les dice a Adán y Eva: "Fructificad y multiplicaos; llenad la tierra y sojuzgadla; y señoread sobre los peces del mar, sobre las aves de los cielos y sobre todas las bestias que se mueven sobre la tierra" (Gén. 1:28). Este mandato se repite y se aclara en la Gran Comisión, cuando Cristo les dice a Sus seguidores que hagan discípulos de todas las naciones. En resumen, el mandato cultural es el encargo dado al hombre como portador de la imagen de Dios de cuidar y conservar el mundo creado, desarrollándolo fielmente de manera que honre a Dios y bendiga a los demás. Se aplica a todas las esferas de la vida, desde decisiones reflexivas y fundamentadas sobre qué y cómo cultivar un campo, hasta deliberaciones fieles y piadosas sobre cómo gobernar un país. Cuando ejercemos un dominio piadoso, el Señor promete derramar Su bendición sobre nuestro trabajo y nuestro mundo (Salmo 72:1-8).

En los siguientes párrafos, quiero tomar el mandato cultural como un mandato general, junto con las promesas en la santa y eterna Palabra de Dios de que toda la tierra será llena de la gloria del Señor, y reflexionar sobre lo que estas cosas significan para nosotros en una esfera cultural en particular: el área del arte y de la creatividad humana.

Definiendo los Términos — Arte y Significado

Sin querer insultar la inteligencia de nadie, comencemos por definir nuestros términos. Para los fines presentes, por "arte" me refiero a las bellas artes en general—el arte visual y cosas relacionadas como la arquitectura y la escultura, así como la música, la poesía, la literatura, la danza, el teatro, y más recientemente, el cine. Esto es para distinguir las bellas artes de las artes liberales. Las artes liberales se llaman así porque, al practicarlas, son las artes que nos ayudan a ser *libres*— artes como la historia, la literatura, la teología y la filosofía—al ayudarnos a entender e interactuar con el mundo. "Bellas" artes simplemente significa artes acabadas; son lo que hacemos como personas libres. En resumen, el propósito principal de las bellas artes no es ser útiles para algún otro fin; es arte por el arte mismo.

Aun así, debajo de todo eso, permanece la pregunta: ¿qué es el arte? Se han escrito libros y se han construido carreras en torno a esta pregunta, pero el filósofo cristiano Calvin Seerveld corta gran parte del ruido ideológico cuando dice que,

> El arte es un asunto mucho menos desconcertante de lo que a menudo se pretende. Para mí, el arte significa estilo. El arte es la objetivación simbólica de ciertos aspectos de significado de una cosa, sujeta a la ley de la alusividad.[1]

Esta es una forma algo técnica de decir que el arte es algo que el hombre crea y que muestra, en lugar de decir, su mensaje. Y se reconoce como "arte" en la medida en que expresa algo verdadero y significativo sobre el mundo. Esto no debería ser controversial, pero a medida que la sociedad occidental comenzó a abandonar su obediencia a Dios y a Su Palabra, también perdimos la comprensión y el consenso sobre lo que califica como arte. Andrew Kern lo explica así: "Antes de la Ilustración, los europeos al menos —y creo que la mayoría de las culturas— usaban el arte para encarnar significados que creían haber identificado en el mundo tal como es." Por lo tanto, si vamos a crear o evaluar arte desde una perspectiva distintivamente cristiana, nuestra crítica se centrará en si una obra de arte da gloria a Dios.

Creatividad Llena del Espíritu

A Dios le importa la belleza — la creación no solo funcionaba, era "buena en gran manera." En su libro *The Mind of the Maker*, la educadora y erudita Dorothy L. Sayers comienza considerando la pregunta "¿qué es el hombre?", y empieza con el relato bíblico de la creación del hombre. Sabemos por este relato que el hombre fue creado a imagen de Dios, y Sayers escribe que, aunque tenemos al hombre, el portador de la imagen, delante de nosotros, en este punto del relato bíblico no se nos dice mucho acerca de cómo es Dios. Si llevamos la imagen de Dios, ¿cuál es exactamente el *contenido* de esa imagen? Sayers observa que lo único que sabemos en este punto de la historia del mundo es que Dios crea, y que lo que Él crea es bueno.[2]

El Catecismo Menor de Westminster enseña que el fin principal del hombre es glorificar a Dios y gozar de Él para siempre. Una de las pruebas bíblicas para esta afirmación es Efesios 2:10, donde Pablo explica a los cristianos de Éfeso que somos hechura de Dios. Como obras de arte nosotros mismos, debemos hacer otras obras de arte, y tanto nosotros como nuestras obras estamos hechos para glorificar. Dar gloria a Dios debe ser el criterio del cristiano para determinar si algo es buen arte, mal arte o no es arte. El universo está lleno de significado, porque la creación depende completamente de la Palabra de Dios que la habló a la existencia y que la sostiene en todo momento. El significado de la creación es señalar y dar gloria al Creador. Esto es verdad tanto de las cosas que Él crea como de las cosas que nosotros, como portadores de Su imagen, creamos.

Otra razón por la que necesitamos el arte es que no podemos ir en contra de nuestra naturaleza dada por Dios. La creatividad está arraigada en lo que significa ser humano, y en el trato de Dios con Su pueblo, esta naturaleza creativa se manifiesta de forma prominente. Considérese este detalle en las instrucciones del Señor a Moisés para construir el tabernáculo en Éxodo 31:

> [1] Y el SEÑOR habló a Moisés, diciendo: [2] Mira, he llamado por nombre a Bezaleel, hijo de Uri, hijo de Hur, de la tribu de Judá. [3] Y lo he llenado del Espíritu de Dios en sabiduría, en inteligencia, en conocimiento y en toda *clase de* arte, [4] para elaborar diseños, para trabajar en oro, en plata y en bronce, [5] y en el labrado de piedras para engaste, y en el tallado de madera; a fin de que trabaje en toda *clase de* labor. [6] Mira, yo mismo he nombrado con él a Aholiab, hijo de Ahisamac, de la tribu de Dan; y en el corazón de todos los que son hábiles he puesto habilidad a fin de que hagan todo lo que te he mandado... (LBLA).

No te pierdas esto: Bezalel y Aholiab fueron llenos del Espíritu de Dios — esto fue un evento muy raro en el Antiguo Testamento, y Dios lo hizo con estos artesanos porque la belleza le importa a Dios. Es una de las formas principales en que damos gloria a Dios.

Por supuesto, no todos están llamados a ser artistas profesionales. Pero el aspecto estético es inalienable a lo que significa ser humano; no podemos evitar crear, y no podemos evitar tener una sensibilidad estética. Si alguna vez elegiste colores de pintura o muebles para tu casa, o zapatos para tus pies, hiciste elecciones estéticas.

Retirada hacia el Compromiso

Cuando los cristianos escuchamos sobre el ámbito contemporáneo del arte, generalmente no lo pensamos como un área particularmente piadosa de la cultura. La mayoría de nosotros piensa en piezas conceptuales escandalosas y aleatorias que nadie entiende, que afirman estar haciendo una declaración profunda sobre algún aspecto de la vida, pero que la mayoría de las veces solo buscan impactar o confundir. Y esto es precisamente lo que deberíamos esperar, porque un artista que no cree que haya orden y significado en la vida reflejará esa creencia en su arte. Así es como terminamos con supuestas exposiciones artísticas que consisten en pedazos rotos de concreto sobre un plato, y un tipo con gafas moradas diciéndonos que es un símbolo de la alienación suburbana.

Si alguna vez has visitado, y especialmente si alguna vez has llevado a un grupo de jóvenes a una exposición como esta, habrás oído un comentario repetido murmurado frente a cada pieza: "Yo podría hacer eso." Este comentario reconoce el problema clave con lo que se llama arte conceptual: el único poder que tiene está en el concepto. El filósofo inglés Roger Scruton, en su documental *Why Beauty Matters*, ilustra bien este punto cuando dice:

> Solo necesitas decir: "media vaca flotando en un tanque de formaldehído" — y ya está. La única habilidad involucrada en esa pieza proviene del carnicero que te da la media vaca. No logras nada adicional al llevar a cabo el concepto en la vida real.[3]

Porque Dios nos diseñó para reconocer y apreciar la verdadera belleza, respondemos con razón a tales exhibiciones con desdén o desprecio. Esta es una respuesta natural, pero en nuestro rechazo a ese tipo de antiarte, debemos tener cuidado de no abandonar toda la esfera del arte.

'Arte Cristiano'

Lamentablemente, esto es exactamente lo que ha ocurrido en gran parte del cristianismo occidental. Creo que los cristianos han abandonado infielmente una parte clave de nuestra herencia legítima, dada por Dios, como portadores de Su imagen, al permitir que los enemigos de Dios controlen las artes. Los cristianos tienen el derecho y la responsabilidad de hacer buen arte, y la triste realidad es que a menudo hemos renunciado a eso; hemos descuidado nuestro deber con respecto al mandato cultural.

En lugar de hacer mejor arte, que glorifique a Dios y que diga algo verdadero sobre el mundo, nos hemos replegado a guetos cristianos donde usamos nuestros clichés cristianos y donde a los incrédulos no les importa lo que hacemos. En lugar de simplemente tratar de hacer buena música, escuchamos a las bandas seculares más populares y luego tratamos de armar una versión cristiana imitadora. Hacemos películas cristianas con tramas pobres que siguen una narrativa de conversión predecible y totalmente irreal.

Andrew Kern describe la escena actual del cine cristiano así:

Las películas hechas por cristianos para el mundo cristiano tienden a presentar el mundo como un lugar donde las personas justas terminan saliéndose con la suya al final. Sufren pruebas y luego terminan victoriosas. Sin embargo, no puedo evitar preguntarme si eso no es engañoso y tal vez falla en prepararnos para la realidad. A veces, la realidad es absolutamente aplastante. Absolutamente, insoportablemente aplastante. Y no se arregla... El cristianismo no aboga por el canal Hallmark... por lo cursi, excesivamente encantador y emocionalmente edificante.

Hemos dejado que los enemigos de Dios construyan y luego monopolicen todas las plataformas mediáticas más grandes, y nos hemos rendido sin dar batalla. A esto es a lo que Douglas Wilson llama una retirada hacia el compromiso. Cedemos el terreno donde se libran las verdaderas batallas culturales, nos agrupamos en un gueto cristiano, y decimos que estamos dando la cara. Actuamos como si fuéramos fieles porque hacemos películas con guiones que hablan sobre la oración, sobre Dios, sobre superar dificultades y hacer todas las cosas por medio de Cristo, pero lo que muchas de estas películas realmente están haciendo es actuar sin fe. La razón por la que gran parte del arte cristiano contemporáneo es mal arte es porque miente sobre Dios al no presentar el mundo de una manera veraz, rehusándose a reconocer que la vida real es desordenada y peligrosa, y a veces no se ajusta en lo más mínimo a nuestros gustos.

El Dios que Habla

Como cristianos, adoramos a un Dios creativo, creador y que habla. Todos los demás dioses son ídolos inútiles. La única razón por la que alguien es creativo es porque Dios nos ha dado la creatividad. Por esta razón, los cristianos debemos rechazar la cobarde mentira de que el arte, la música y el cine del incrédulo son el estándar; debemos dejar de asumir que el mundo es mejor en esto y dejar de tomar ejemplo del mundo en nuestra propia expresión creativa. Debemos recordar que llevamos la imagen de nuestro Creador, y que tenemos al Espíritu Santo, quien nos guía a toda verdad, y debemos hacer arte que refleje esa realidad.

Notas Finales

1.   Calvin Seerveld, "A Look at Books," *The Outlook Magazine*, 1963, p. 39.

2.   Dorothy L. Sayers, *The Mind of the Maker*, London: Methuen, 1941, p. 3.

3.   Roger Scruton. *Why Beauty Matters*. Directed by Paul G. Allen. 2009. London: BBC, 2009.

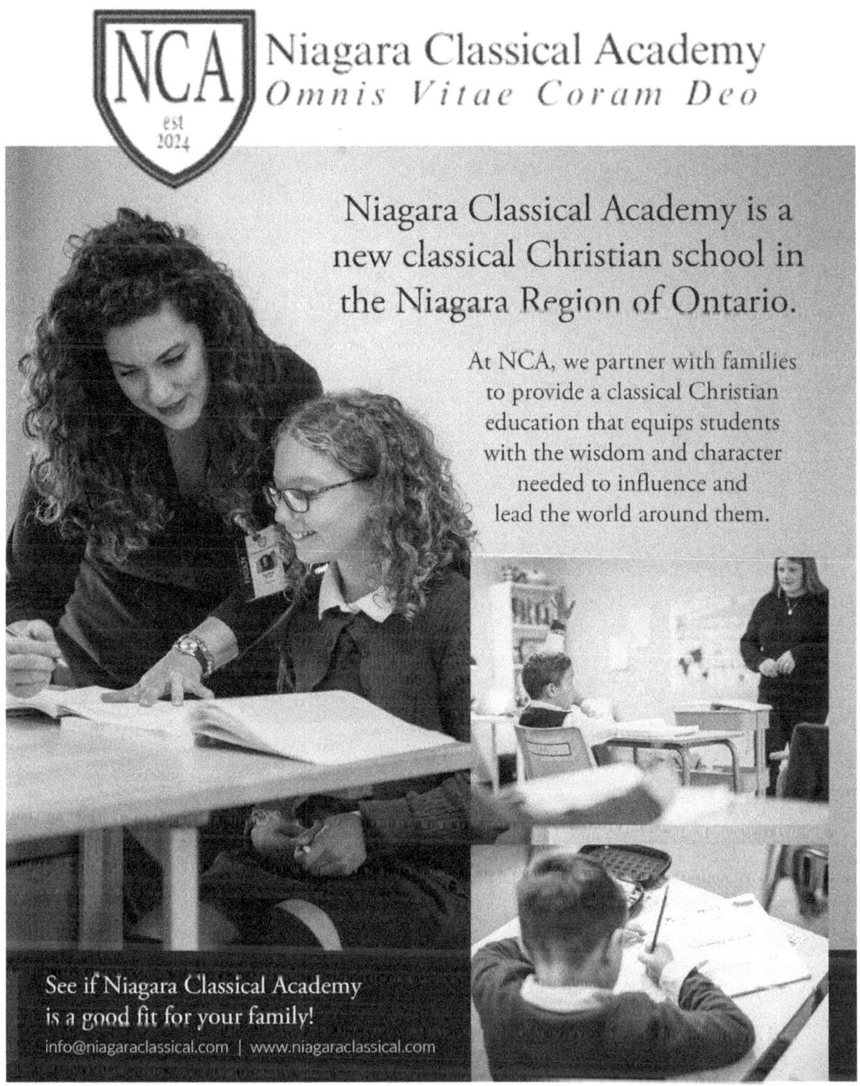

Traducción: La Niagara Classical Academy es una nueva escuela cristiana clásica en la región del Niágara, Ontario. En NCA, colaboramos con las familias para brindar una educación cristiana clásica que forme a los estudiantes con la sabiduría y el carácter necesarios para influir y liderar en el mundo que los rodea. ¡Descubre si Niagara Classical Academy es una buena opción para tu familia!

Human Responses to Art: Good, Bad, and *Indifferent*

by Calvin G. Seerveld

Editorial Note: *The following is a transcript of the opening lecture originally delivered at a conference organized by the faculty and student body of Dordt College on November 5–6, 1981. The conference featured performances in theatre, dance, and music, each followed by critical discussion. In addition, visual art and film were presented and subsequently subjected to critique. Permission for its republication was attained from the author and Dordt College.*

I SHOULD LIKE TO begin with an appropriate paragraph from Revelation 18:21-24:

> And one strong angel picked up a rock, big as a millstone, and heaved it into the lake, saying: That's the way—boom!—the great city of Babylon shall get the heave and never be found again. The sound of guitarists and folk singers and flutists and trumpeters shall nevermore be heard in your city; no artist, in any of the arts, shall be found any more in your great city. The sound of the millstone grinding shall be heard among you no more forever, and the lamp-light shall shine no more among you forever, and the voice of bridegroom and bride shall nevermore be heard among you, nevermore—your businessmen were the bigshots of the earth!—nevermore, because all the people were misled by your clever artistry. They found blood too in that city Babylon, blood of prophets and saints and all those believers who were butchered to death on the earth.[1]

Art by its presence demands a response from you as a human person

In our culture today, whether you live in Sioux Center, Toronto, or New York City, you are confronted by art. Even if you don't read, you still go to the movies. If you close your eyes, you still hear somebody's transistor radio with its mix of music and commercials. If you should use ear plugs and a seeing-eye dog, you would still feel the pattern of city streets as you ride in the back of a taxi, or sense the architectural shape of the building you are entering as you walk through a revolving door. Art by its ubiquitous presence demands your response, even if its rejection.

The Bible is concerned that our response be filled with a holy spirit that knows what is good and what is evil so that what we sense, see performed, read, hear, and understand does not poison or butcher us. The Bible wants us to learn how to be edified and compassionately deepened by what we perceive, so that we know and exercise what is important for a child of God (cf. Titus 1:15, Philippians 1:9-11).

That is our topic: we are examining the human response to art. By way of introduction let me say that this is a very complicated problem. When a Dordt theater-arts major and a farmer go to the same play, they *see* the same performance very differently. It's up to the theater-arts department, the *Diamond*, and the Public Relations department of the college to mediate those different perceptions. Even though they are looking at the same canvases, a Christian Reformed Church ladies-aid looks at a Matheis art show much differently than would Clement Greenberg, the New York art critic. And the direction of the art department at Dordt depends upon which perceptions the leaders take seriously. When a talent scout for the Chicago Symphony and an almost tone-deaf, prospective donor for musical instruments listens to the Dordt orchestra, they *hear* very differently the same sounds.

I'm not talking "good guys" versus "bad guys," as if there were an elect elite and a reprobate mass of people responding to art. In fact, I tend to trust the naïve person more than the sophisticated one, particularly if the simple person is a Bible-believing Christian, unaffected by TV, who wants to serve God on earth. I'm simply trying to show you that there are many subjective factors at work in the experience of artistic events and art-works. A dramatist should be aware that there may be farmers in his audience; a mid-western artist needs to know about the New York art scene, and the Dordt choir must realize that few people can actually hear the intricate structure of a madrigal. But our focus now is on the farmer, the city critic, and church audience—how should one respond to art? And can we examine it in a way that acknowledges that one and the same art object will occupy (briefly) the attention of a wide variety of people?

This problem can be made concrete in connection with this lecture. If you are an educational philosophy student required to attend and take notes, it affects what you hear. If you just dropped in, know nothing about art, but are interested in being educated, you will *hear* things differently. Now the philosophical question is: how do people receive artworks, performance, and books of short stories? Are there right ways for people to experience art which will unlock its flavor and meaning? What are the key problems theorists (have to) take a stand on with regard to seeing, hearing, and reading of art?

Marxist, Freudian, or Idealist theories of response-to-art will mislead us in regard to our perception of art.

As a Christian thinker I would say, first of all, that one should beware of over-simplified answers, and test the spirit in the theory of response-to-art you examine. A Marxist approach normally curses the middle class WASP (White Anglo-Saxon Protestant) enjoyment of a piece of art as a smug evil, and blesses all those who demand that art be a useful weapon for stamping out injustice in society. A Freudian approach tends to advocate "letting yourself go" at a concert. Since art for the Freudian is essentially a substitute for sex, the simulated orgasms at a punk-rock festival are much better for emotional stability than the polite, inhibited applause after a cantata at First Church. An Idealist theory focuses on the idea-content of an art-work—if you get that, you've got it all; anything more is either gravy or distraction.

What I am saying is that a carefully thought-out response to art assumes a theory of art as well as a theory of knowledge, a philosophy of perception. If you take art to be a therapeutic stimulus or a sugar-coated idea, propaganda or a luxury item like chocolate cake, you will experience art within that defining framework. I know that artworks normally have a point and always mean something, and that the emotion-stretching component of art is very important, and that art objects show the artist's commitment to be or not to be societally responsible. But an Idealist, Freudian, or Marxist theory of response-to-art each over-exposes its cherished elements and therefore misleads by blocking out other crucial factors, thereby warping perceptions of art into an ideological rut.

The task of a Christian theory of aesthetics, and also of a Christian theory of perception, would be to set out the key features of a normative, aesthetic response-to-art. It should also spell out pivotal factors one should look for, listen to, and wait for in the various art forms, so that we will be saved from one-sided short-sighted, and other wrong responses. A Christian response-to-art; nevertheless, a theory of aesthetics, if it embodies Christian insight, can help grind the lenses for the eye-glasses and temper the diaphragms of the earphones of your art-experience.

Thesis: For us not to respond to art as a piece of *art*, imaginatively, is to miss the meaning of its artistry.

A human creature should respond to art in kind if he or she intends to make the dated acquaintance of artworks in God's world. A piece of art is a piece of art. Art is not a stimulus to nerve endings; it is not an instrument to complete a plan; it is not a signpost, nor a mathematical problem to be figured out and solved. A piece of music or theater or a painting normally is stimulating and formed to get something across; an artwork usually says something and needs to be understood. But its stimulating, constructed, signifying, and thought-provoking come-ons are features of its character as an *art-object*. An artwork or an artistic performance must be responded to first of all *imaginatively* or you miss its meaning. Artworks are *imaginatively* stimulating, *imaginatively* formed, *imaginatively* discussible, *imaginatively* thoughtful. That's what an art work is, if it is art—an object made to be known and responded to imaginatively by human subjects in God's world.

Inadequate Reactions

In my judgment this means it is inadequate to respond to a choreographed dance by only saying, "I like it," or "I don't like it." Don't get me wrong: it's okay to have likes and dislikes. Likes and dislikes are rooted in our God-given sensitivity to pleasure and pain. But if our chief response to a ballet movement is, "It turns me on," or "It turns me off," then we have a very undeveloped, not to say stunted, response to an artwork. To be chiefly turned-on or turned-off by art as a person is not very intelligent activity. Such a stance mistakenly treats an art object as if it were akin to a body rub or a cold shower.

A more involved and common but still inadequate reception of art is conveyed by the exclamation "Neat-o!" or "Cool, man!" Such judgments often prize the skill displayed—for example, the sheer virtuosity of the guitar-playing by Jimi Hendricks recorded in the film *Woodstock*. This kind of response, inadequate though it may be, requires inside knowledge of technique. One responds to a musical performance as one responds to a good double-play in baseball or an expert, delayed-pass routine in football. One can't put it into a lot of words, maybe, but you are enough of a rock or Bach buff to know the finesse or slightest error in fingering or intonation. You admire or disapprove the act with cold-blooded,

arm-chair professionalism. This kind of specialist-trained ear or eye—and it often is not academically trained—is personified in the knowing look and hip-language sign of approval or the kind of cutting remark heard sometimes at intermission: "The horns were flat in the second movement." If this is the limit or the focus of listening to music, then pieces of music are treated not as artworks, but primarily as technical operations.

Over-reaching Responses

Next to these two kinds of inadequate, mistaken art-receptions, which I'll call the *grunt reaction* and the *umpire perception*. I'd like to mention briefly a couple of others which overshoot the mark, you might say, instead of reducing art to stimulus for a grunt or to a trick worth watching to see whether it's a ball or a strike.

Some people are inclined to meet theater or cinema, for example only at the verbal level. They read movie reviews and after they've gone, can talk a blue streak about what the actors did, describe in detail episode after episode in a film, tell you the story line, the message, and specify its contents clearly. Very literate. But such a literate recounting of *Equus* or *Clockwork Orange* seems untouched by a poignance of make-believe human horses with heads and hooves of empty, shiny metal, or by the distorted, looming, ants-eye camera shot of the rape and the lurking presence of Beethoven's *Ninth* in the soundtrack. This is a talkative way of seeing and hearing, of experiencing a play or film, that tends to overlook and miss the exact nuances most difficult to translate into words. The person seems satisfied with what can be paraphrased. So one could identify this kind of misfocus as the *paraphrastic response.*

Another kind of approach to artworks or artistic performance is with a lattice-work, as it were, thrown up in front of your face that allows you to see only what can be precisely, analytically put away. You treat a painting as if it's in a laboratory and you are dissecting it, probing each element microscopically for germs of thought, examining and explaining all the casual connections you can rustle up, staying alert for any ideas there may be, but discounting what is not conceptually interesting as the packaging one needs to unwrap. Aestheticians, psychologists, philosophers, and university graduate students who are not careful may err this way when they leave the classroom and go to a concert or an art gallery or read a novel. Applying a the-

oretical grid straight-away to a Bach fugue, a Moore sculpture, or Watteau painting pre-empts their experiencing in all its lovely polyphonic or polysemous ambiguity. This overreaching approach to artwork I'd call *scientistic attention.*

So far I've been reporting on what I think are inadequate and over-reaching ways to perceive artworks—four mistaken kinds of ways of responding to artistic presentations. There are more wrong ways to confront artworks, which do not respond to art in kind, but I'll let them go for now (cf. *A Christian Critique of Art and Literature,* p. 107, n. 3). But let me make two notes to head off misunderstandings until I can get more of the whole picture spelled out.

(1) You will seldom find pure, air-tight specimens of these mistaken types of art reception. We respond inadequately as human creatures, but the Lord graciously compensates for us, keeps us from totally ruining our lives when we have a severe case of Gruntitis or Umpire pox or suffer from Paraphrastic diarrhea. It's not even the end of the world if we're struck down by Scientistic fever, although all these wrong ways to respond to art will be a curse of sorts on us and the

artists, closing us down and putting a whammy on certain real, creaturely joys. Also, please realize I am not saying there should be a taboo on feeling, know-howing, talking, and thinking when we respond to artworks. In fact, without feeling or know-how, the correct response to art will be weak, and I'll argue that talking and thinking are crucial for a deepened perception of art. The point I'm coming to is that the sensing, know-howing, describing, and thinking activities must be submerged within an *imaginative openness* to the art object. All these normal, operating activities must become functions fused within the act of response which is focused on the piece of art or artistic performance in its *nuances*. All important functions of the response-to-art activity must be focused by the art object's defining quality of allusivity.

(2) It's entirely legitimate to analyze a Hopkins' poem like "God's Grandeur" or to decide whether you want to pay thirty dollars to see Peter Schafer's play *Amadeus* off-Broadway. It's fair enough to decide whether you like or dislike Steve Reich's music or whether the colors of a Picasso print will match or clash with the wallpaper in your living room—fair enough! If you are willing to respect the art-ob-

ject character of the artwork in question. In the respects I've just mentioned, artworks are no different from a ton of coal, which you may or may not like to have in your living room either, with its dust or smell. That is, artworks exist in the world along with tons of mined coal, which is also a cultural object needing to be responded to by men and women *as mined coal* in a number of ways—analysis, price, fitting in with your living room or not. And it's utterly legitimate to make human decisions on these sorts of external relations of artworks and of coal. So it's fair enough to say, "I don't want my kids to see Tantric temple sculpture," and "The price tag on a Rembrandt is as immoral as what Steinbrenner will pay to sew up a slugger in a Yankee uniform"—fair enough. There are all kinds of contexts in which artworks find themselves which need Christian concern and where non-artistic judgments are valid—about the art, or coal. But right now we are trying to recognize how to appreciate, pick up, notice, understand an artwork or artistic event in its *artistic* meaning, its particularly artistic character, which is intrinsic to the nature of artistry like painting, music, theater, and cinema.

Imaginative Reading of an Art Object or of Artistic Meaning

The prime feature of a human act of response to an artwork is an intent awareness of the pregnant allusiveness of the piece. I should like to contend that the way to get at the aesthetic quality which, for me, defines an art object is that one activate its congealed nuances. And the only way to activate the nuanced meaning which the artist, and performers as co-artists, have brought to an artistic head is to read it nuancefully. That's what I take an imaginative response to be: a nuanceful reading that plays perceptively and intelligently with the nuances of anything. Since an artwork, in my understanding, is always a humanly crafted object that is at its core virtually a metaphor—visual, aural, worded, gestural, or whatever—since a Rouault painting, a Brahms concerto, Ionesco's *Rhinoceros* or *Macbett* is a qualitatively nuanced artifact of symbolific compression, then an imaginative reading is what it takes to make the art object come alive as an artwork.

Let me explain that. By "imaginative reading" I mean an intuitional retracing of the art object. You play back in your consciousness whatever the pasty, stained-glass colors and heavy,

leaden, black smudges of lines in Rouault's painting of Christ's head suggest, and you mull over the hidden meanings hovering all around and within the images; but you leave it wonderfully shadowy. Or you replay in your consciousness as it takes place the opening scenes of Bergman's staging of Gombrowicz' drama *Yvonne, Princess of Burgundy*, where you'd swear the 1920s-dressed courtiers of the king look like two-dimensional, cardboard props in a ritzy, furniture show window, and you store the caricatured gestures of those puppet people, as an index to their cramped violence—you pick up and keep those telling nuances percolating subliminally while they build imaginatively with a compounding complicity. Or you play along in your consciousness with the sight-sound metaphor of Yehudi Menuhin directing his select string orchestra in a concert performance of Boyce, Mozart, Bartok, and Haydn, and you thrill, with eighteenth-century decorum, at the nicety of the symmetrical musical phrases, the relatively simple melodic patterns, the reassuringly constant tempo that allows such clean virtuosity in subtle changes of timbre and tones—you listen and hear indirectly a world of elegance, arabesques, make-believe and frolic.

A nuanced reading of an art object—whether a painting, theatrical piece, or symphony—seeks to imagine how the sensible, constructed, and allusion-rich composition comes to mean what it does; and your thoughtfully sensitive awareness remains at an intuited kind of retrieval. No matter whether your imaginative knowing is experienced and deep or tentative and beginning, an imagining-active playback (and I didn't say "feedback") of the art object in all its fused symbolic penumbras of meaning remains curious, prone to re-reading the piece, full of wonder.

An imaginative reading of an art object does not exhaust itself in sense-perception, and it does not aim at a comprehensive understanding that wraps up the piece. There is a genuinely more-than-visible yet unfinished-off ambiguity that is integral and structurally permanent, I think, to an imaginative reception of art because (1) that's the defining way an art object is, and (2) that's the right way to perceive, conceive, receive art—what Kant was trying to pin down with "taste" and "aesthetic judgment," what Susanne K. Langer means by "intuitive discernment of non-discursive import," and what Rudolph Arnheim explores in "visual thinking."

Symbolify: the Professional Norm for Making Art

We're coming to the heart of my remarks now; so we'll go more slowly.

First, the art object. It takes hypersensitive, skill-trained people to lay the foundation for making a piece of sculpture or for composing a sonata. (I know there are all kinds of borderline cases of people who are not overly sensitive nor very skillful who come up with a good song or poem in their lifetime, but things are so complicated we've got to take clear-cut examples.) If you are insensitive to the properties of clay and cannot "think with your hands," as the expression goes, you will make a poor sculptor or potter. If you have no ear for music and are sloppy at organization, you will have trouble composing a piece for six musical instruments to play that will hold attention for more than five minutes. You don't have to be married or be a Christian or be twenty years old to be a bona fide artist, but you do need, in my book, to show a certain measure of crafting ability in a medium, be it of clay or tones or words or whatever. Being able to design in a medium is the base line, I think, for producing an artwork which deserves the name of art.

An artist also needs a special kind of insight, an aesthetic discernment and imaginative ability to capture meanings at large and transform them, meta-morphose them, into a suggestion-rich entity which not only keeps all the delicate shades of suggestion-rich meaning intact, but also somehow has enough integrality and durance to be an object made precisely for aesthetic imaginative attention. That's what I use the terms "symbolical" and "symbolical objectification" to describe. An art object is the objectified presentation of certain (other) meanings which a subjective artist has crafted so that its very being-there is of "symbolical" quality—allusiveness permeates its whole existence. An art object is like an alluring, ambiguous wink hinting at matters worth experiencing, full of knowledge bottled for those who can open up its allusiveness and taste it—aesthetically. So "symbolical" means for me in the context of aesthetic theory "a professionally fashioned and honed allusiveness." "Symbolical objectification" and "symbolify" are short phrases for describing the most salient feature of artistic activity.

Lots of things could be added: (a) how art objects can be a professional service to help people become more aware of nuances in ordinary, non-artistic circumstances of life. I want to make people aware that art is relevant for all of life—it can open our eyes and ears to creatural glories, if it's right—and I'd like to reform Christianly the idea of professional. To be a professional artist should mean you unblushingly profess the committed mold to your whole life in your artistry, and you believe that what you are being is worthy of mastery—"professional." Such an idea would curb the evil of uncommitted professionalism and would also encourage amateur artists. Every artist who earns his or her living by his artistry began as an apprentice once upon a time. Even "professional" responders-to-art began as amateurs!—and amateur artists don't need to make it full-time work. But they are called, I believe, to do justice to whatever they take up as an artistic hobby, that is, take its "symbolical" nature seriously, rather than just mess around therapeutically—which would have a different rationale.

(b) Those of you who have read *Rainbows for the Fallen World* know that I understand practical jokes and surprises as *aesthetic* objects or events, also typified by allusiveness (pp. 49-59) which can be as real, important, and memorable as many a painting or poem. But unlike *artistic* objects, which are professionally "symbolified" artifacts, aesthetic objects are more effervescent and meshed with shifting societal contexts, it seems to me. So if nobody gets the joke or surprise, maybe it wasn't there, but if nobody gets the play or the musical composition, it's still more there somehow than the intended joke was.

(c) The history of reflection on "symbol" can be investigated at length until finally you take your own stand somewhere and try to use the term wisely. "Symbolical" for me is the norm for art. Symbolical, as I said, is the allusive feature heightened professionally, the allusive squared, you might say, or taken to a higher power of refinement. So a "symbol" is different from a sign, which signifies something clearly. An "=" is not a symbol in my vocabulary: it is a mark designating mathematical identity or logical similarity. Words too are essentially signs, pointers, with a syntactic framework and a range of meaning even though words have a built-in symbolic layer—their connotations. When English sentences are turned into poetry, the connotations take the lead, incorporate and overshadow the denotations; so poetry is less clear language than ordinary sentences because it has become symbolically heightened language.

"Symbolical," then, is the criterion for whether something is art or not. Whether an artifact or handicraft is art or propaganda, art or the exercise of an expert, and so on, depends on whether its defining characteristic is symbolical. I know people will differ in judging a particular event. People even differ on whether "symbolical" is the norm for artistic structure. The same is true for deciding whether or not a given act belongs to a biblically Christian life-style. But we may not abdicate a stand because of Christian disunity. We need to posit, in community, imperatives for which the Lord holds us responsible, also in artistry and aesthetic theory, if that is our office; otherwise we forfeit "feeding the sheep" of the Lord. As theorist at this stage of my development I am willing to stand by "symbolical" as the decisive factor for art.

Nuanceful Lineaments of Certain Arts

I still want to offer as pertinent for exploring our responses to artworks like paintings, pieces of music, theater and cinema, an incomplete, a playfully philosophical checklist of artistic features that will reward and can deepen our imaginative perception, conceptual notice, and judgment surrounding our aesthetic reading of specific art objects.

When you face a painting, you do well to look for its nuances of color and try to imagine how the nuances of the painting's constitutive properties such as size, foreground-background, surface-texture (i.e., brush strokes, palette-knife gobs, air-gun sheen) and the nuances of its hues and design contribute to what it, as a whole, symbolifies. Also, try to discover intuitively how simple or complex it is with respect to other painterly dimensions: does it depict? Are there emblems? Are there recurrent motifs in the artist's paintings which allude to a peculiar novelty of interest? You do well to become imaginatively aware of how tasteful and engaging its symbolical quality is and how nuanced the thrust of the piece is, if you want to plumb its artistic meaning.

When you listen properly to music, you need to hear and recognize its musicality. You need to hear the nuances of especially its rhythms. Constitutive properties of music include its tempo and loudness, its vertical pitch patterns and silences. You need to become aware of the pregnant emphases and intended oddities of

phrasing, intensity (i.e., the attack, sustenance, and decay of sound), the nuances of timbre and delicacies of orchestration, for all contribute to the allusive-squared meaning of the music. Aesthetic listening to instrumental music will be enriched if you can intuitively be aware of the expressive, innovative, entertaining and cherished tonal nuances—all the lineaments that make up the symbolical thrust of the piece.

I'm fairly certain that professionals in theater and cinema arts could delineate features that might help harness our habits of perception and intelligence to a more imaginative reading of such artworks and artistic performances too. But let me make my most careful comments about the imaginative response to art. I want to make these comments after having given those sketchy lists of artistic features in paintings and music. We may need to study and learn how to respond to art beyond the grunt and slogan level, but art response must not become scholastic. Art response deserves to be imaginatively deep and aesthetically rich.

A Partial Diagnosis of Imaginative Reception of Artworks

To receive film, novel, cantata, choreographed dance, or a drawing imaginatively, we must perceive the work without losing its impact and richness through a pre-emptive analysis. Nevertheless, to experience the richness of that perception, we must be aesthetically sensitive and artistically aware of the different lineaments of the artwork. Gush kills taste, and expertise can paralyze imaginative perception; but we will not enter the music or the painting or the play aesthetically without empathy, without perception that can simulate and remember intuitively the technical founding elements of the artwork.

Also, to read an art object imaginatively and naturally we shall come to interpret and compare forms. It is a natural tendency for our aesthetic playback of the artwork to put into words and into concepts what we are aesthetically undergoing, to show we are indeed whole people who are discriminating viewers, and listeners able to express what we experience intuitively. But that normal tendency of our imaginative reading to become expressive and discriminating must

not slip into the realm of disinterested description and explanation, because then one rides roughshod over the symbolic qualification of the art and its proper reading, and substitutes talk and thought for imagining. Art criticism, analysis which delves and exposits and distinguishes facts predominantly by simulating and comparing, can develop the calibre of one's primary aesthetic responses to artworks. Art interpretation which highlights and points to symbolical distortions and imaginative over- and under-exposures can facilitate sound art reception. But art criticism and art commentary cannot take the place of original art reception and imaginative reading of the symbolically qualified piece of gifted human artistry.

I would like to develop an aesthetic theory and philosophy of perception that would save you from imaginative paralysis when you face artworks and artistic performances. I want to respond as a child of God who is called to rule this culture in God's Name. It's a Romanticist lie that thinking and speaking about art necessarily kills art reception: to be dumb and blank-minded and filled with a turmoil of inexpressible emotions is not the state of imaginative reading. But it is also a lie that we need to bring this irrational art some decent reasoning. I have tried; or at least clip its wings with some decent reasoning. I've tried to say "No" to both of these responses. I've posited that aesthetic activity has its own prime ontological structure and task interwoven in human life, especially in responding to art.

In closing, just a double note that's important to me: (1) Because every artwork has a date and a tradition and inescapably carries around in itself like a ghost the spirited perspective of its human makers, to read the work accurately, we must see the spirited perspective embedded in that very sensible, crafted, allusion-rich artifact. Many humanistic theories of response to art block out the question of whether art has this horizon of final commitment in its flesh and blood. And too few would-be Christian theories of response to art are willing to confess the sobering fact that at bottom one's response to art is going to meet the question of whether one is faced with what serves the Truth or the Enemy. Powerful art—and that could mean the power of established tradition! Rather than banks of amplifiers—will butcher believers in the last days. In fact, in our technocratic day, art is a more simple and attractive idol than science to many (cf.

Matthew 24:22-24 also). Therefore, we need to taste, sense, perceptively enjoy, remember, interpret, compare, and especially read artworks imaginatively with passages like Matthew 7:1-2, 1 John 4:1, Philippians 1:9-11 giving us the cue. No snap, self-righteous aesthetic judgments will do, but imaginative testing of the spirits of those pieces of art. We must be in the sure grip of the Holy Spirit so that our very sensation knows the overflowing single-minded love of Jesus Christ.

(2) When we visit the theater or attend a musical performance, we will likely be a motley crew, from anti-music auditors, indifferent receivers, partisan fans, and emoting grunters, to professional art-expert listeners, inexpert theorists, psychology professors, and maybe even one or two good imaginative readers of theater and music. What could pull us together would be a unifying, normative sense of what we are responding to (a symbolified object) and a communal working conception of how we can thoughtfully perceive and sensitively think within our (imaginative) response to what goes on as it reaches out to us. That is an edifying, methodical program, I think, of how to proceed.

But I'll make a provocative comment in the hope it will be picked up: to look or hear, perceive and respond to an artwork or artistic performance as if it is itself not *historically embedded*, just as we art-receivers are, is like trying to guess the meaning of a quote out of context, often a foreign-language quote at that. We American Christian academicians—speaking for myself—have often sinned, I think, by treating artworks as if they never grew in historical dirt, as if they grew in an antiseptic laboratory of art formation. But an artwork is truly historically dated and contexted, and we must allow it the time to let the historical context of an artwork worm itself slowly into our experience, informing us of the world it breathed and breathes. Otherwise we interpret the art object according to what ails us. We may delight in Mozart's music so much because its genial loveliness entices us to escape from our secular rush of deadlines, strikes, and machines going on the blink, and thus we may overhear and dismiss its rococo spirit. Or we may falsify artworks and sterilize imaginative responses in our performance practices when we bring artworks to the stage with little regard to historical setting. The striking difference between concert and theater programs in München, London, and New York makes my point. The German program holds a short, reflective essay in layman's language, giving the historical setting of the piece and something of its afterlife. The British program gives a few art critical remarks about significant features of the work. The American *Playbill* lists the cast with their credits and many advertisements of other shows in town and nothing else—you're on your own.

My closing remark for this session is to ask each of us to realize that when we examine human response to art and try to delineate its proper structure, we are only treating the abc's of an art response. But I'm glad we're doing it, because it's important to grasp even the abc's of factors in art response with the innocent circumspection of Christ's proverbial dove and snake (Matt. 10:16).

Working Bibliography

The Aesthetic Eye: Generative Ideas. Eds. F.D. Hine, Ronald Silverman et altera. The National Endowment for the Humanities & Office of the Los Angeles County Superintendent of Schools, 1976. v-57.

Arnheim, Rudolf. *Visual Thinking.* Los Angeles: U. of California Press, 1969. Second paperback edition, 1972. xi-345.

Barzun, Jacques. *The Use and Abuse of Art.* 1973. Princeton University Press paperback, 1975. 150pp.

Blanshard, Frances Bradshaw. *Retreat from Likeness in the Theory of Painting.* New York: Columbia University Press, 1949. x-178.

Brooks, Cleanth. *The Well Wrought Urn.* New York: Harcourt, Brace & World Harvest paperback, 1947. xiv-300.

Broudy, Harry S. *Enlightened Cherishing. An essay on aesthetic education.* Urbana: University of Illinois Press, 1972. 120 pp.

Bullough, Edward. "'Psychical Distance' as a factor in art and an aesthetic principle" (1912) in *Art and Philosophy. Readings in aesthetics.* Ed. W.E. Kennick. New York: St. Martin's Press, 1966. pp. 534-51.

Buytendijk, F.J.J. *Prolegomena van een antropologische fysiologie.* Utrecht: Aula-boeken, 1965. 350 pp.

Casey, Edward S. *Imagining. A phenomenological study.* Bloomington: Indiana University Press, 1976. xvi-240.

de Graaff, Arnold H. *Psychology: sensitive openness and appropriate reactions.* Potchefstroom University for CHE, 1980. 23pp.

Ehrenzweig, Anton. *The Hidden Order of Art.* Berkeley: University of California Press, 1967, first paperback edition, 1971. xiv-306 ± 30 plates.

Gibson, James J. "A theory of pictorial perception," in *Sign, Image, Symbol.* Ed. Gyorgy Kepes. New York: George Braziller, 1966. pp. 92-107.

Gombrich, E.H. "Oh physiognomic perception" (1960) in *Meditations on a Hobby Horse.* London: Phaidon, third edition, 1978. pp. 45-55.

Greene, Theodore Meyer. *The Arts and the Art of Criticism.* Princeton University Press, 1940. xxxii-690.

Guggenheimer, Richard. *Sight and Insight. A prediction of new perceptions in art* (1945). Port Washington, New York: Kennikat Press Inc., 1968. ix-246.

Lanz, Henry. "Aesthetic relativity," in *Stanford University Publications University Series: Language and Literature* 7 (no. 1, 1947): 3-20.

Lipps, Theodor. "Einfühlung, inner Nachahmung, und Organempfindungen," *Archiv für die gesamte Psychologie* 1 (no. 1, 1903): 185-204.

Lipps, Theodor. "Zur ästhetischen Mechanik," *Zeitschrift für Ästhetik und Allgemeine Kunstwissenschaft* 1 (1906): 1–29.

Schapiro, Meyer. "Mr. Berenson's values," *Encounter* 16 (January 1961): 57–65.

Schwartzman, Helen B. "Research on Children's Play: an overview, and some predictions," in *Proceedings of the Association for the Anthropological Study of Play* (1977). Ed. Michael A. Salter. West Point: Leisure Press, 1978. pp. 105–15.

Seerveld, Calvin. *A Christian Critique of Art and Literature* (1964). Toronto: Association for the Advancement of Christian Scholarship, second edition, 1977. 127pp.

Seerveld, Calvin. "A christian tin-can theory of man," *Journal of the American Scientific Affiliation* 33 (July 1981): 74–81.

Seerveld, Calvin. *Rainbows for the Fallen World. Aesthetic life and artistic task.* Toronto: Tuppence Press, 1980. 254 pp.

Sibley, Frank N. "Aesthetic concepts," *Philosophical Review* 68 (October 1959): 421–50.

Springer, Sally P. & Georg Deutsch. *Left Brain, Right Brain.* San Francis-co: W.H. Freeman & Co., 1981. xii–243.

Steensma, G.J. & Harro W. van Brumme-len. eds. *Shaping School Curriculum, a biblical view.* Terre Haute, Indiana: Signal Publishing Co., 1977. 178pp.

Tashiro, Tom. "Ambiguity as aesthetic principle," in *Dictionary of the History of Ideas.* New York: Charles Scribner's Sons, 1973. 1:48–60.

Wolterstorff, Nicholas. *Art in Action.* Grand Rapids: Wm. B. Eerdmans, 1980. x-240.

Zuidervaart, Lambert. Chapter 1, "Introduction," in *Kant's Critique of Beauty and Taste: Explorations into a philosophical aesthetics.* Toronto: Institute for Christian Studies, M. Phil. thesis, 1977. pp. 1–16.

Endnotes

1.   Translation my own from the Greek.

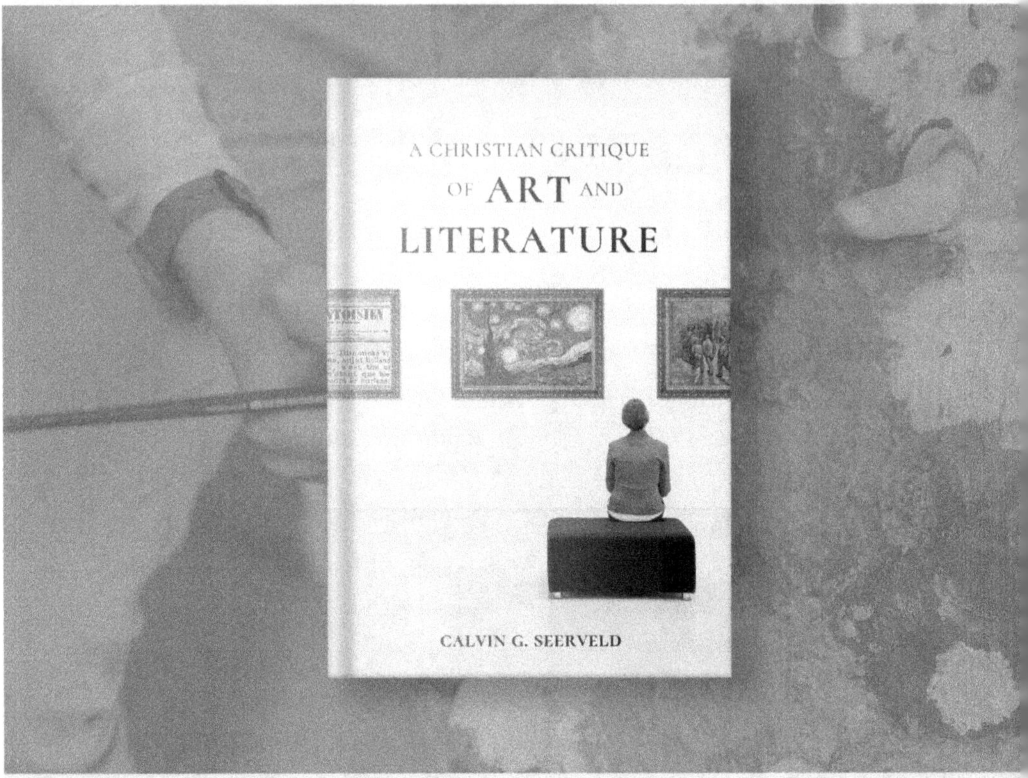

Respuestas Humanas al Arte: *Buenas, Malas y Indiferentes*

por Calvin G. Seerveld

Nota Editorial: *Lo siguiente es una transcripción de la conferencia inaugural presentada originalmente en un congreso organizado por el cuerpo docente y estudiantil de Dordt College los días 5 y 6 de noviembre de 1981. El congreso incluyó presentaciones de teatro, danza y música, cada una seguida de una discusión crítica. Además, se exhibieron obras de arte visual y cine, las cuales también fueron sometidas a análisis crítico. Se obtuvo el permiso para su publicación por parte del autor y de Dordt College.*

QUISIERA COMENZAR con un párrafo apropiado de Apocalipsis 18:21-24:

Y un ángel poderoso levantó una piedra, grande como una piedra de molino, y la arrojó al mar, diciendo: Así—¡zas!—la gran ciudad de Babilonia será derribada y jamás se la volverá a encontrar. El sonido de guitarristas y cantantes, de flautistas y trompetistas, jamás volverá a oírse en tu ciudad; ningún artista, de ningún arte, se encontrará ya más en tu gran ciudad. El sonido de la piedra de molino moliendo no se oirá jamás entre ustedes, y la luz de la lámpara no brillará más en ti, y la voz del esposo y de la esposa jamás volverá a oírse en ti—¡tus comerciantes eran los grandes magnates de la tierra!—pero nunca más, porque todo el pueblo fue engañado por tu astuta creatividad. Y también hallaron sangre en esa ciudad Babilonia, sangre de profetas y de santos y de todos los creyentes que fueron masacrados en la tierra.[1]

El arte, por su sola presencia, exige una respuesta de ti como persona humana

En nuestra cultura actual, ya sea que vivas en Sioux Center, Toronto o Nueva York, estás constantemente confrontado con el arte. Aun si no lees, igual vas al cine. Si cierras los ojos, igual escuchas la radio de alguien con su mezcla de música y anuncios comerciales. Si usas tapones para los oídos y un perro guía, aún percibirías el patrón de las calles de la ciudad mientras vas en la parte trasera de un taxi, o sentirías la forma arquitectónica del edificio al que entras al pasar por una puerta giratoria. El arte, por su presencia ubicua, exige tu respuesta, incluso si esa respuesta es el rechazo.

La Biblia se preocupa de que nuestra respuesta esté llena de un espíritu santo que sepa discernir entre lo bueno y lo malo, para que lo que percibimos, vemos representado, leemos, oímos y comprendemos no nos envenene ni nos destruya. La Biblia desea que aprendamos a ser edificados y profundizados con compasión por lo que captamos, de modo que sepamos y practiquemos lo que es importante para un hijo de Dios (cf. Tito 1:15; Filipenses 1:9–11).

Ese es nuestro tema: estamos examinando la respuesta humana al arte. A modo de introducción, permítanme decir que se trata de un problema muy complejo. Cuando un estudiante de teatro de Dordt y un agricultor asisten a la misma obra, ambos presencian la misma función, pero la perciben de manera muy distinta. Corresponde al departamento de teatro, al *Diamond* (el periódico estudiantil), y al departamento de Relaciones Públicas de la universidad mediar entre esas percepciones tan diferentes. Aunque estén observando los mismos lienzos, un grupo de damas de la Iglesia Reformada Cristiana percibe una exposición de Matheis de manera muy distinta a como lo haría Clement Greenberg, el crítico de arte neoyorquino. Y la orientación que tome el departamento de arte de Dordt dependerá de cuáles de esas percepciones sus líderes consideren importantes. Del mismo modo, cuando un buscador de talentos de la Sinfónica de Chicago y un posible donante casi sin oído musical escuchan a la orquesta de Dordt, ambos *oyen* los mismos sonidos, pero los interpretan de forma muy diferente.

No estoy hablando de "los buenos" contra "los malos", como si existiera una élite escogida y una masa reprobada de personas que responden al arte. De hecho, tiendo a confiar más en la persona ingenua que en la sofisticada, especialmente si esa persona sencilla es un cristiano que cree en la Biblia, no está influenciado por la televisión y desea servir a Dios en la tierra. Lo que intento mostrar simplemente es que hay muchos factores subjetivos en juego en la experiencia de eventos y obras artísticas. Un dramaturgo debería estar consciente de que puede haber agricultores en su audiencia; un artista del medio oeste necesita conocer la escena artística de Nueva York; y el coro de Dordt debe darse cuenta de que pocas personas pueden captar realmente la estructura intrincada de un madrigal. Pero ahora nos enfocamos en el agricultor, el crítico urbano y la audiencia eclesiástica: ¿cómo debería uno responder al arte? ¿Y podemos examinar esta cuestión reconociendo que una misma obra de arte puede captar (por un momento) la atención de una gran diversidad de personas?

Este problema puede concretarse en relación con esta misma conferencia. Si eres un estudiante de filosofía de la educación obligado a asistir y tomar apuntes, eso afecta lo que *escuchas*. Si simplemente entraste por curiosidad, sin saber nada de arte pero con interés en aprender, escucharás las cosas de forma distinta. Ahora bien, la pregunta filosófica es: ¿cómo reciben las personas las obras de arte, las presentaciones, o los libros de cuentos? ¿Existen formas correctas de experimentar el arte que permitan liberar su sabor y significado? ¿Cuáles son los problemas clave sobre los cuales los teóricos deben tomar una postura en cuanto a la manera de ver, oír y leer el arte?

Las teorías marxistas, freudianas o idealistas sobre la respuesta al arte pueden desorientarnos en cuanto a nuestra percepción del arte

Como pensador cristiano, diría ante todo que uno debe cuidarse de las respuestas simplistas y poner a prueba el espíritu de la teoría sobre la respuesta al arte que se esté examinando. El enfoque marxista suele maldecir el disfrute del arte por parte de la clase media protestante anglosajona (WASP) como un mal arrogante, y bendecir a todo aquel que exija que el arte sea un arma útil para erradicar la injusticia social. El enfoque freudiano tiende a promover el "dejarse llevar" en un concierto. Como para el freudiano el arte es esencialmente un sustituto del sexo, los orgasmos simulados en un festival de punk-rock son mucho mejores para la estabilidad emocional que los aplausos educados y reprimidos tras una cantata en la Primera Iglesia. La teoría idealista, por su parte, se enfoca en el contenido intelectual de la obra de arte—si uno capta eso, lo ha entendido todo; todo lo demás es un añadido o una distracción.

Lo que estoy diciendo es que una respuesta bien pensada al arte presupone tanto una teoría del arte como una teoría del conocimiento, es decir, una filosofía de la percepción. Si entiendes el arte como un estímulo terapéutico, una idea disfrazada de dulzura, una pieza de propaganda o un lujo como una torta de chocolate, entonces experimentarás el arte dentro de ese marco interpretativo. Yo sé que las obras de arte normalmente tienen un propósito y siempre significan algo, y que el componente emocional del arte es muy importante, y que las obras artísticas reflejan el compromiso del artista de asumir o no una responsabilidad social. Pero una teoría marxista, freudiana o idealista de la respuesta al arte exagera sus propios elementos favoritos y, por lo tanto, termina desorientando al bloquear otros factores fundamentales, deformando así la percepción del arte dentro de una rutina ideológica.

La tarea de una teoría cristiana de la estética, y también de una teoría cristiana de la percepción, consiste en exponer los elementos clave de una respuesta estética normativa al arte. Esta teoría también debe señalar los factores fundamentales que uno debe buscar, escuchar y esperar en las distintas formas artísticas, para que podamos ser librados de respuestas unilaterales, miopes y equivocadas. Una respuesta cristiana al arte—es decir, una teoría estética que encarne una visión cristiana—puede ayudar a pulir los lentes de nuestros anteojos y afinar los diafragmas de los auriculares de nuestra experiencia artística.

Tesis: No responder al arte como *arte*, es decir, de manera imaginativa, es perder el significado mismo de su arte.

Una criatura humana debe responder al arte en su misma naturaleza si pretende entablar una relación genuina con las obras artísticas en el mundo de Dios. Una obra de arte es una obra de arte. El arte no es un simple estímulo para las terminaciones nerviosas; no es un instrumento para completar un plan; no es un cartel indicador, ni un problema matemático que deba resolverse. Una pieza musical, teatral o pictórica normalmente es estimulante y está compuesta con la intención de comunicar algo; una obra de arte por lo general dice algo y necesita ser comprendida. Pero su carácter estimulante, su forma construida, su capacidad de significar y provocar pensamiento son rasgos de su identidad como *objeto artístico*. Una obra o una interpretación artística debe ser recibida, ante todo, con *imaginación*, o se perderá su verdadero significado. Las obras de arte son estimulantes desde lo *imaginativo*, están formadas *imaginativamente*, se prestan al diálogo *imaginativo* y al pensamiento *imaginativo*. Eso es lo que constituye una obra de arte, si verdaderamente lo es: un objeto hecho para ser conocido y respondido con imaginación por sujetos humanos en el mundo de Dios.

Reacciones Inadecuadas

A mi juicio, esto significa que no es adecuado responder a una danza coreografiada simplemente diciendo: "Me gusta" o "No me gusta". No me malinterpretes: está bien tener gustos y disgustos. Los gustos y disgustos están arraigados en nuestra sensibilidad dada por Dios al placer y al dolor. Pero si nuestra respuesta principal ante un movimiento de ballet es: "Me enciende" o "Me apaga", entonces tenemos una respuesta muy poco desarrollada,

por no decir atrofiada, ante una obra de arte. Dejarse llevar principalmente por la excitación o la repulsión ante el arte no es una actividad muy inteligente. Tal postura trata erróneamente una obra de arte como si fuera un masaje corporal o una ducha fría.

Una recepción del arte más común y participativa, aunque igualmente inadecuada, se expresa con exclamaciones como "¡Qué chévere!" o "¡Qué bacán!" Estos juicios a menudo valoran la destreza demostrada—por ejemplo, la pura virtuosidad de la guitarra de Jimi Hendrix grabada en la película *Woodstock*. Este tipo de respuesta, aunque limitada, requiere cierto conocimiento interno de la técnica. Se responde a una interpretación musical como se responde a una buena jugada doble en béisbol o a una jugada experta con pase retrasado en fútbol. Tal vez no se pueda poner en muchas palabras, pero uno es lo suficientemente aficionado al rock o a Bach como para notar la destreza o el más mínimo error en el digitado o en la entonación. Se admira o se desaprueba el acto con un profesionalismo frío y de sillón. Este tipo de oído o mirada entrenada—que muchas veces no es académica—se personifica en la mirada cómplice y el lenguaje "cool" de aprobación, o en ese tipo de comentario mordaz que se escucha a veces durante el intermedio: "Los metales estaban desafinados en el segundo movimiento." Si este es el límite o el enfoque al escuchar música, entonces las piezas musicales no se tratan como obras de arte, sino principalmente como operaciones técnicas.

Respuestas Exageradas

Junto a estos dos tipos de recepciones inadecuadas o erróneas del arte—las que podríamos llamar la *reacción gruñona* y la *percepción de árbitro*—me gustaría mencionar brevemente un par más que, por así decirlo, se pasan de la raya. En lugar de reducir el arte a un estímulo que provoca un gruñido o a una destreza digna de ver solo para juzgar si fue bola o strike, estas respuestas lo sobreintelectualizan.

Algunas personas tienden a enfrentarse al teatro o al cine, por ejemplo, solo desde el plano verbal. Leen reseñas de películas y, después de haberlas visto, pueden hablar largo y tendido sobre lo que hicieron los actores, describir con detalle episodio tras episodio, contar la trama, el mensaje, y especificar su contenido con claridad. Muy cultos, sin duda. Pero este relato tan letrado de *Equus* o *La naranja mecánica* parece no haber sido tocado por la conmoción que provoca el fin-

gimiento de caballos humanos con cabezas y pezuñas de metal brillante y vacío, o por el plano distorsionado, desde la perspectiva de una hormiga, de la violación, acompañado por la presencia inquietante de la Novena de Beethoven en la banda sonora. Es una forma habladora de ver y oír, de experimentar una obra o película, que tiende a pasar por alto y perder las sutilezas más difíciles de traducir en palabras. La persona parece satisfecha con lo que puede ser parafraseado. Así que podríamos identificar este tipo de desenfoque como la *respuesta parafrástica*.

Otro tipo de acercamiento a las obras o representaciones artísticas consiste en levantar, por así decirlo, una especie de enrejado frente al rostro que solo permite ver lo que puede ser analizado y clasificado con precisión. Se trata la pintura como si estuviera en un laboratorio, disecándola, sondeando cada elemento con lupa en busca de gérmenes de pensamiento, examinando y explicando todas las conexiones causales que uno pueda reunir, manteniéndose alerta ante cualquier idea que surja, pero descartando aquello que no resulta conceptualmente interesante como si fuera solo el envoltorio que hay que quitar. Estetas, psicólogos, filósofos y estudiantes de posgrado universitario que no tienen cuidado pueden caer en este error al salir del aula para ir a un concierto, una galería de arte o leer una novela. Aplicar de inmediato una cuadrícula teórica a una fuga de Bach, una escultura de Moore o una pintura de Watteau impide experimentar la obra en toda su hermosa ambigüedad polifónica o polisémica. A este enfoque desmedido ante una obra de arte lo llamaría *atención cientificista*.

Hasta ahora he estado comentando lo que considero formas inadecuadas y desmedidas de percibir las obras de arte—cuatro maneras erróneas de responder a las presentaciones artísticas. Existen más formas equivocadas de enfrentarse al arte, que no responden al arte en su propia índole, pero por ahora las dejaré de lado (cf. *A Christian Critique of Art and Literature*, p. 107, n. 3). Sin embargo, permítanme hacer dos observaciones para evitar malentendidos mientras logro exponer una imagen más completa.

(1) Rara vez se encontrarán ejemplos puros y herméticamente cerrados de estos tipos erróneos de recepción artística. Respondemos de manera inadecuada como criaturas humanas, pero el Señor, en Su gracia, nos compensa, y no permite que arruinemos por completo nuestras vidas cuando sufrimos un caso severo de *gruñitis*, de *viruela arbitral*, o padecemos de *diarrea parafrástica*. Ni siquiera es el fin del mundo si nos derriba la *fiebre cientificista*, aunque todas estas formas incorrectas de responder al arte serán, en cierto sentido, una maldición tanto para nosotros como para los artistas, pues nos cierran el corazón y nos lanzan un maleficio contra ciertos gozos reales de criaturas. Asimismo, por favor entiendan que no estoy diciendo que debamos imponer un tabú sobre el sentir, el saber hacer, el hablar o el pensar al responder al arte. De hecho, sin sentir o sin pericia, la respuesta correcta al arte será débil, y sostendré que el hablar y el pensar son esenciales para una percepción más profunda de la obra. El punto al que quiero llegar es que el sentir, el saber hacer, el describir y el pensar deben estar sumergidos dentro de una apertura *imaginativa* hacia el objeto artístico. Todas estas actividades normales y operantes deben convertirse en funciones fundidas dentro del acto de respuesta, que esté enfocado en la pieza de arte o en la representación artística con todas sus *sutilezas*. Todas las funciones importantes en la actividad de responder al arte deben quedar enfocadas por la cualidad definitoria de la obra artísti-

ca: su *alusividad*.

(2) Es completamente legítimo analizar un poema de Hopkins como *La grandeza de Dios*, o decidir si uno quiere pagar treinta dólares para ver *Amadeus*, la obra de Peter Shaffer, fuera de Broadway. También es válido decidir si te gusta o no la música de Steve Reich, o si los colores de una litografía de Picasso combinan o chocan con el papel tapiz de tu sala—¡perfectamente válido! Siempre y cuando estés dispuesto a respetar el carácter de *objeto artístico* de la obra en cuestión. En los aspectos que acabo de mencionar, las obras de arte no son distintas de una tonelada de carbón, que tal vez tampoco quieras tener en tu sala, ya sea por el polvo o el olor. Es decir, las obras de arte existen en el mundo junto con toneladas de carbón extraído, que también es un objeto cultural al que los hombres y mujeres deben responder de varias maneras: análisis, precio, adecuación o no al entorno del hogar. Y es absolutamente legítimo tomar decisiones humanas respecto a estas relaciones externas de las obras de arte—y del carbón. Así que está bien decir: "No quiero que mis hijos vean esculturas tántricas de templos" o "El precio de un Rembrandt es tan inmoral como lo que Steinbrenner pagaría por asegurar a un bateador estrella con

el uniforme de los Yankees"—válido también. Existen muchos contextos en los que las obras de arte se encuentran y que requieren una preocupación cristiana, y donde los juicios no artísticos son válidos—ya sea sobre el arte o sobre el carbón. Pero en este momento estamos intentando reconocer cómo apreciar, captar, notar, entender una obra de arte o un evento artístico *en su significado artístico*, en su carácter propiamente artístico, que es intrínseco a la naturaleza misma del arte como la pintura, la música, el teatro o el cine.

Lectura Imaginativa de un Objeto de Arte o de su Significado Artístico

La característica principal de un acto humano de respuesta ante una obra de arte es una atención intencional a la *alusividad preñada* de la pieza. Me atrevería a afirmar que la forma de acceder a la cualidad estética que, para mí, define un objeto artístico es activando sus matices condensados. Y la única manera de activar ese significado matizado que el artista, y los intérpretes como co-artistas, han llevado a su expresión artística culminante es leerlo con matices. Eso es lo que entiendo por una respuesta imaginativa: una lectura matizada que juega de forma perceptiva e inteligente con los matices de cualquier cosa. Ya que una obra de arte, según mi entendimiento, es siempre un objeto fabricado humanamente que en su esencia es virtualmente una metáfora—visual, sonora, verbal, gestual o lo que sea—ya que una pintura de Rouault, un concierto de Brahms, *El rinoceronte* o *Macbett* de Ionesco son artefactos cualitativamente matizados de *compresión simbólica*, entonces lo que se requiere para que el objeto artístico cobre vida como obra de arte es una *lectura imaginativa*.

Permítanme explicar eso. Por "lectura imaginativa" me refiero a un *re-trazado intuicional* del objeto artístico. Uno reproduce en su conciencia todo lo que sugieren los colores pastosos, como vitrales, y las gruesas manchas negras de líneas en la pintura de la cabeza de Cristo de Rouault, y reflexiona sobre los significados ocultos que flotan dentro y alrededor de las imágenes; pero los deja maravillosamente en penumbra. O uno reproduce en su mente, a medida que se desarrolla, las escenas iniciales del montaje de Bergman de la obra *Ivonne, princesa de Borgoña* de Gombrowicz, donde uno juraría que los cortesanos del rey, vestidos como en los años veinte, parecen decorados bidimensionales, como de cartón, en una vitrina lujosa de muebles, y guarda los gestos caricaturescos de esos personajes-marioneta como un índice de su violencia reprimida—uno capta y conserva esos matices reveladores que siguen filtrándose subliminalmente mientras se van acumulando imaginativamente con una complicidad creciente. O uno sigue en su conciencia la metáfora visual-sonora de Yehudi Menuhin dirigiendo a su orquesta de cuerdas selecta en un concierto con obras de Boyce, Mozart, Bartók y Haydn, y se deleita, con decoro dieciochesco, ante la elegancia de las frases musicales simétricas, los patrones melódicos relativamente simples, el tempo tranquilizadoramente constante que permite una virtuosidad tan limpia en los cambios sutiles de timbre y tono—uno escucha y percibe indirectamente un mundo de elegancia, arabescos, fantasía y juego.

Una lectura matizada de un objeto artístico—ya sea una pintura, una obra teatral o una sinfonía—busca imaginar cómo la composición sensible, construida y cargada de alusiones llega a significar lo que significa; y tu conciencia, reflexiva y sensible, permanece en un tipo de recuperación intuida. No importa si tu conocimiento imaginativo es experimentado y profundo o si está apenas en sus comienzos; la reproducción activa e imaginativa (y no dije "retroalimentación") del objeto artístico, con todas sus penumbras simbólicas fundidas, permanece curiosa, abierta a nuevas relecturas, llena de asombro.

Una lectura imaginativa de una obra de arte no se agota en la percepción sensorial, ni busca un entendimiento total que agote la pieza. Hay una ambigüedad verdaderamente *más que visible* y sin cerrar, que considero integral y estructuralmente permanente en la recepción imaginativa del arte, porque (1) así es, por definición, una obra de arte, y (2) así es como debe ser percibida, concebida y recibida—eso que Kant intentó precisar con los conceptos de "gusto" y "juicio estético", lo que Susanne K. Langer llama "discernimiento intuitivo de un contenido no discursivo", y lo que Rudolf Arnheim explora bajo el nombre de "pensamiento visual".

Simbolificar: la Norma Profesional para Hacer Arte

Estamos llegando al corazón de mis observaciones; así que avanzaremos más lentamente.

Primero, el objeto artístico. Se necesita de personas hipersensibles y con formación técnica especializada para sentar las bases que permitan crear una escultura o componer una sonata. (Sé que hay todo tipo de casos fronterizos—personas que no son particularmente sensibles ni muy hábiles pero que logran escribir una buena canción o poema en algún momento de su vida—pero dado lo complejo del asunto, necesitamos partir de ejemplos claros). Si eres insensible a las propiedades del barro y no puedes "pensar con las manos", como suele decirse, serás un mal escultor o alfarero. Si no tienes oído musical y eres desorganizado, tendrás dificultades para componer una obra para seis instrumentos musicales que logre captar la atención por más de cinco minutos. No hace falta estar casado, ni ser cristiano, ni tener veinte años para ser un artista legítimo; pero, en mi opinión, sí es necesario mostrar cierto nivel de habilidad en el manejo de un medio, ya sea barro, sonidos, palabras o lo que sea. Tener la capacidad de diseñar en un medio es, creo, el requisito básico para producir una obra que merezca ser llamada arte.

El artista también necesita un tipo especial de percepción—un discernimiento estético y una capacidad imaginativa para captar significados dispersos y transformarlos, *metamorfosearlos*, en una entidad rica en sugerencias que no solo conserve todos los matices delicados de sentido, sino que además posea la integridad y consistencia necesarias para ser un objeto creado *precisamente* para la atención estética e imaginativa. Eso es lo que intento describir con los términos *simbólico* y *objetivación simbólica*. Una obra de arte es la presentación objetivada de ciertos significados (otros) que un sujeto-artista ha plasmado de tal forma que su misma presencia posee una cualidad *simbólica*—una *alusividad* que impregna todo su ser. Un objeto artístico es como una guiñada seductora y ambigua que insinúa realidades dignas de ser experimentadas, cargadas de conocimiento embotellado para quienes saben abrir su alusividad y saborearla—*estéticamente*. Así que *simbólico* significa para mí, en el contexto de la teoría estética, *una alusividad profesionalmente elaborada y afinada. Objetivación simbólica y simbolificar* son expresiones abreviadas para describir el rasgo más destacado de la actividad artística.

Hay muchas cosas que podrían añadirse: (a) cómo los objetos artísticos pueden prestar un servicio profesional ayudando a las personas a volverse más conscientes de los matices presentes en las circunstancias ordinarias y no artísticas de la vida. Deseo hacer ver que el arte es relevante para toda la vida—puede abrir nuestros ojos y oídos a las glorias de la

creación, *si es correcto*—y me gustaría reformar, cristianamente, la idea de lo profesional. Ser un artista profesional debería significar que uno profesa sin vergüenza alguna un compromiso que moldea toda su vida mediante el arte que practica, y que cree que aquello que está siendo y haciendo merece ser considerado digno de *maestría*—eso es ser "profesional." Esta noción corregiría el mal del profesionalismo sin compromiso, y al mismo tiempo animaría a los artistas aficionados. Todo artista que hoy vive de su arte empezó alguna vez como aprendiz. ¡Incluso los "profesionales" que responden al arte comenzaron siendo aficionados!—y no todo artista aficionado necesita convertirlo en un trabajo de tiempo completo. Pero creo que están llamados a hacer justicia a aquello que asumen como pasatiempo artístico, es decir, a tomar en serio su carácter *simbólico*, en lugar de simplemente usarlo con fines terapéuticos—lo cual, claro está, respondería a una lógica distinta.

(b) Quienes han leído *Rainbows for the Fallen World* saben que entiendo las bromas y las sorpresas como objetos o eventos estéticos, también caracterizados por su alusividad (pp. 49‑59), que pueden ser tan reales, importantes y memorables como muchas pinturas o poemas. Pero a diferencia de los objetos *artísticos*, que son artefactos profesionalmente "simbolificados", los objetos estéticos son, en mi opinión, más efervescentes y entrelazados con contextos sociales cambiantes. Así que, si nadie capta la broma o la sorpresa, tal vez no estaba allí; pero si nadie capta la obra teatral o la composición musical, de algún modo todavía *sí* está allí.

(c) La historia de la reflexión sobre el "símbolo" puede investigarse extensamente hasta que uno finalmente toma una postura propia e intenta usar el término con sabiduría. "Simbólico", para mí, es la norma del arte. Simbólico, como dije, es la característica alusiva llevada a su máxima expresión profesional; la *alusividad al cuadrado*, por así decirlo, o llevada a una potencia superior de refinamiento. Así que un "símbolo" es distinto de un signo, que significa algo de forma clara. Un "=" no es un símbolo en mi vocabulario: es una marca que designa identidad matemática o similitud lógica. Las palabras también son esencialmente signos, indicadores, con una estructura sintáctica y un rango de significado, aunque tienen una capa simbólica incorporada—sus connotaciones. Cuando las oraciones en inglés se convierten en poesía, las connotaciones toman el liderazgo, incorporan

y ensombrecen las denotaciones; por eso la poesía es un lenguaje menos claro que las oraciones comunes, porque se ha convertido en un lenguaje *simbólicamente intensificado*.

"Simbólico", entonces, es el criterio para determinar si algo es arte o no. Si un artefacto o una artesanía es arte o propaganda, arte o ejercicio de un experto, etc., depende de si su característica definitoria es simbólica. Sé que las personas diferirán al juzgar un evento en particular. Incluso difieren en si lo "simbólico" es la norma para la estructura artística. Lo mismo ocurre al decidir si un acto determinado pertenece o no a un estilo de vida bíblicamente cristiano. Pero no podemos abdicar nuestra postura debido a la desunión cristiana. Debemos, en comunidad, establecer imperativos por los cuales el Señor nos hace responsables, también en el ámbito del arte y la teoría estética, si ese es nuestro oficio; de lo contrario, renunciamos a "alimentar a las ovejas" del Señor. Como teórico, en esta etapa de mi desarrollo, estoy dispuesto a sostener que lo *simbólico* es el factor decisivo para el arte.

Lineamientos Matizados de Ciertas Artes

Todavía deseo proponer, como algo pertinente para explorar nuestras respuestas ante obras de arte como pinturas, piezas musicales, teatro y cine, una lista incompleta—filosófica en tono y lúdica en intención—de rasgos artísticos que pueden enriquecer y profundizar nuestra percepción imaginativa, nuestra atención conceptual y nuestro juicio en torno a la lectura estética de objetos artísticos específicos.

Cuando te enfrentas a una pintura, conviene buscar sus matices de color e intentar imaginar cómo las propiedades constitutivas de la obra—como su tamaño, la relación entre primer plano y fondo, la textura superficial (es decir, pinceladas, empastes con espátula, brillos de pistola de aire), así como los matices de sus tonos y diseño—contribuyen a lo que simboliza como un todo. Asimismo, intenta descubrir intuitivamente cuán simple o compleja es respecto a otras dimensiones pictóricas: ¿representa algo? ¿Hay emblemas? ¿Aparecen motivos recurrentes en las obras del artista que aluden a una peculiar novedad de interés? Es recomendable volverse imaginativamente consciente de cuán refinada y atractiva es su cualidad simbólica, y cuán matizado es el impulso de la pieza, si uno desea ahondar en su significado artístico.

Cuando escuchas música adecuadamente, necesitas oír y reconocer su musicalidad. Necesitas percibir especialmente los matices de su ritmo. Las propiedades constitutivas de la música incluyen su tempo y volumen, los patrones verticales de tono y los silencios. Es necesario volverse consciente de los énfasis cargados de sentido y de las rarezas intencionadas en las frases musicales, de la intensidad (es decir, el ataque, la duración y la desaparición del sonido), de los matices de timbre y de las sutilezas de la orquestación, pues todo ello contribuye al significado *alusivo al cuadrado* de la música. La escucha estética de la música instrumental se verá enriquecida si uno puede captar intuitivamente los matices tonales expresivos, innovadores, encantadores y entrañables—todos los rasgos que constituyen el impulso simbólico de la pieza.

Estoy bastante seguro de que los profesionales en las artes del teatro y el cine podrían delinear características que también ayudarían a encauzar nuestros hábitos de percepción e inteligencia hacia una lectura más imaginativa de tales obras y representaciones artísticas. Pero permítanme ahora hacer mis comentarios más cuidadosos sobre la *respuesta imaginativa al arte*. Quiero hacerlos después de haber ofrecido esas listas esquemáticas de rasgos artísticos en la pintura y la música. Puede que necesitemos estudiar y aprender a responder al arte más allá del nivel del gruñido o del eslogan, pero la respuesta al arte no debe volverse escolástica. La respuesta artística merece ser *profundamente imaginativa* y *estéticamente rica*.

Diagnóstico Parcial de la Recepción Imaginativa de las Obras de Arte

Para recibir de manera imaginativa una película, una novela, una cantata, una danza coreografiada o un dibujo, debemos percibir la obra sin perder su impacto y riqueza mediante un análisis prematuro. Sin embargo, para experimentar verdaderamente la riqueza de esa percepción, es necesario ser estéticamente sensibles y artísticamente conscientes de los distintos *lineamientos* de la obra. El entusiasmo desbordado arruina el buen gusto, y la pericia técnica puede paralizar la percepción imaginativa; pero no entraremos en la música, la pintura o la obra teatral *estéticamente* sin empatía, sin una percepción capaz de simular y recordar intuitivamente los elementos técnicos fundantes de la obra.

Además, al leer un objeto artístico de manera imaginativa y natural, llegaremos inevitablemente a *interpretar y comparar formas*. Es una tendencia normal en nuestra reproducción estética del objeto artístico *poner en palabras y en conceptos* lo que estamos experimentando estéticamente—para mostrar que somos personas íntegras, espectadores y oyentes capaces de discriminar y expresar lo que experimentamos intuitivamente. Pero esa tendencia normal de nuestra lectura imaginativa a volverse expresiva y analítica *no debe derivar* en una descripción o explicación desapasionada, porque entonces se atropella la cualificación simbólica del arte y su lectura adecuada, sustituyendo la *imaginación* por el *discurso* y el *pensamiento*.

La crítica de arte—ese análisis que indaga, expone y distingue hechos predominantemente mediante la simulación y la comparación—puede desarrollar la calidad de nuestras respuestas estéticas primarias ante las obras. La interpretación artística que destaca y señala las distorsiones simbólicas y las sobreexposiciones o subexposiciones imaginativas puede facilitar una recepción saludable del arte. Pero ni la crítica de arte ni el comentario artístico pueden sustituir la *recepción artística original* ni la *lectura imaginativa* de la obra dotada de cualificación simbólica, fruto de la creatividad humana.

Deseo desarrollar una teoría estética y una filosofía de la percepción que te libre de la parálisis imaginativa al enfrentarte a obras y representaciones artísticas. Quiero responder como un hijo de Dios, llamado a gobernar esta cultura en el Nombre de Dios. Es una mentira del romanticismo que pensar y hablar sobre el arte necesariamente arruine la recepción del arte: quedarse mudo, en blanco, y lleno de un torbellino de emociones inexpresables *no* es el estado de una lectura imaginativa. Pero también es mentira que debamos someter este arte "irracional" a un razonamiento respetable; o, al menos, recortarle las alas con razonamientos decentes. Yo he intentado decir "no" a ambas respuestas. He planteado que la actividad estética tiene su propia estructura ontológica fundamental y su tarea, entretejidas en la vida humana, especialmente en la respuesta al arte.

Para concluir, una doble nota que para mí es importante:

(1) Dado que toda obra de arte tiene una fecha y una tradición, y que inevitablemente lleva consigo como un fantasma la perspectiva animada de sus creadores humanos, para leerla con precisión debemos ver esa perspectiva espiritual incrustada en ese artefacto

sensible, elaborado y lleno de alusiones. Muchas teorías humanistas de la respuesta al arte excluyen de entrada la pregunta de si el arte encarna o no un horizonte de compromiso final en su carne y sangre. Y muy pocas teorías cristianas de la respuesta al arte están dispuestas a confesar el hecho sobrio de que, en el fondo, toda respuesta al arte se enfrenta a la cuestión de si uno está ante algo que sirve a la *Verdad* o al *Enemigo*.

El arte poderoso—¡y eso puede significar el poder de una tradición consagrada más que bancos de amplificadores!—despedazará creyentes en los últimos días. De hecho, en nuestra época tecnocrática, el arte se ha convertido en un ídolo más simple y atractivo que la ciencia para muchos (cf. Mateo 24:22–24 también). Por tanto, debemos *saborear, percibir, gozar con discernimiento, recordar, interpretar, comparar*, y sobre todo *leer* las obras de arte *imaginativamente*, con pasajes como Mateo 7:1–2, 1 Juan 4·1 y Filipenses 1:9–11 como guía. No bastan juicios estéticos precipitados ni autosuficientes, sino una *prueba imaginativa de los espíritus* de esas obras. Debemos estar en el *seguro dominio del Espíritu Santo*, de modo que *nuestros mismos sentidos* conozcan el desbordante y firme amor de Jesucristo.

(2) Cuando visitamos el teatro o asistimos a una presentación musical, probablemente seamos un grupo heterogéneo: desde auditores antimúsica, receptores indiferentes, fanáticos partidarios y entusiastas emotivos, hasta oyentes expertos en arte, teóricos inexpertos, profesores de psicología, y quizá uno o dos buenos lectores imaginativos del teatro y la música. Lo que podría unirnos sería un sentido normativo y unificador de aquello a lo que estamos respondiendo (un objeto simbolificado), y una concepción de trabajo común sobre cómo podemos percibir con discernimiento y pensar con sensibilidad dentro de nuestra respuesta *imaginativa* a lo que se nos presenta. Me parece que este es un programa edificante y metódico para proceder.

Pero haré un comentario provocador con la esperanza de que se recoja: mirar o escuchar, percibir y responder a una obra artística como si no estuviera ella misma históricamente enraizada—tal como lo estamos nosotros, los receptores del arte—es como intentar adivinar el significado de una cita fuera de contexto, y a menudo de una cita en lengua extranjera. Nosotros, los académicos cristianos estadounidenses—hablando por mí mismo—hemos pecado, creo, al tratar las obras de arte como si no hubieran crecido en la tierra de la historia, como si hubieran sido cultivadas en un laboratorio antiséptico de formación artística. Pero una obra de arte está verdaderamente *fechada* y *contextualizada históricamente*, y debemos concederle el tiempo necesario para que su contexto histórico se infiltre lentamente en nuestra experiencia, informándonos sobre el mundo que respiró y aún respira. De lo contrario, interpretamos el objeto artístico según nuestras propias dolencias. Puede que nos deleite la música de Mozart porque su encanto alegre nos invita a escapar de nuestras prisas seculares, huelgas y máquinas averiadas, y por ello pasamos por alto o desechamos su espíritu rococó. O quizá falseamos las obras de arte y esterilizamos nuestras respuestas imaginativas en la práctica escénica cuando llevamos obras al escenario sin tener en cuenta su contexto histórico. La diferencia llamativa entre los programas de conciertos y teatro en Múnich, Londres y Nueva York ejemplifica mi punto. El programa alemán incluye un breve ensayo reflexivo en lenguaje sencillo, que ofrece el contexto histórico de la obra y algo sobre su recepción posterior. El programa británico aporta algunos comentarios críticos sobre rasgos significativos de la pieza.

El *Playbill* estadounidense enumera el reparto con sus créditos y una gran cantidad de anuncios de otros espectáculos en la ciudad—y nada más: estás por tu cuenta.

Mi comentario final para esta sesión es pedirnos a cada uno que reconozcamos que, al examinar la respuesta humana al arte e intentar delinear su estructura adecuada, no estamos haciendo más que tratar con el *abecé* de la respuesta artística. Pero me alegra que lo estemos haciendo, porque es importante comprender incluso ese *abecé* de los factores que intervienen en la respuesta al arte con la *circunspección inocente* de la paloma y la serpiente del proverbio de Cristo (Mateo 10:16).

Bibliografía de Trabajo

The Aesthetic Eye: Generative Ideas. Editado por F.D. Hine, Ronald Silverman et al. The National Endowment for the Humanities & Office of the Los Angeles County Superintendent of Schools, 1976. v–57.

Arnheim, Rudolf. *Visual Thinking.* Los Ángeles: University of California Press, 1969. Segunda edición en rústica, 1972. xi–345.

Barzun, Jacques. *The Use and Abuse of Art.* 1973. Edición en rústica de Princeton University Press, 1975. 150 pp.

Blanshard, Frances Bradshaw. *Retreat from Likeness in the Theory of Painting.* Nueva York: Columbia University Press, 1949. x–178.

Brooks, Cleanth. *The Well Wrought Urn.* Nueva York: Harcourt, Brace & World Harvest, edición en rústica, 1947. xiv–300.

Broudy, Harry S. *Enlightened Cherishing: An Essay on Aesthetic Education.* Urbana: University of Illinois Press, 1972. 120 pp.

Bullough, Edward. "'Psychical Distance' as a Factor in Art and an Aesthetic Principle" (1912), en *Art and Philosophy: Readings in Aesthetics.* Editado por W.E. Kennick. Nueva York: St. Martin's Press, 1966. pp. 534–551.

Buytendijk, F.J.J. *Prolegomena van een antropologische fysiologie.* Utrecht: Aula-boeken, 1965. 350 pp.

Casey, Edward S. *Imagining: A Phenomenological Study.* Bloomington: Indiana University Press, 1976. xvi–240.

de Graaff, Arnold H. *Psychology: Sensitive Openness and Appropriate Reactions.* Potchefstroom University for CHE, 1980. 23 pp.

Ehrenzweig, Anton. *The Hidden Order of Art.* Berkeley: University of California Press, 1967. Primera edición en rústica, 1971. xiv–306 + ±30 láminas.

Gibson, James J. "A Theory of Pictorial Perception," en *Sign, Image, Symbol.* Editado por Gyorgy Kepes. Nueva York: George Braziller, 1966. pp. 92–107.

Gombrich, E.H. "Oh physiognomic perception" (1960), en *Meditations on a Hobby Horse.* Londres: Phaidon, tercera edición, 1978. pp. 45–55.

Greene, Theodore Meyer. *The Arts and the Art of Criticism.* Princeton University Press, 1940. xxxii–690.

Guggenheimer, Richard. *Sight and Insight: A Prediction of New Perceptions in Art* (1945). Port Washington, Nueva York: Kennikat Press Inc., 1968. ix–246.

Lanz, Henry. "Aesthetic relativity," en *Stanford University Publications. University Series: Language and Literature* 7 (n.º 1, 1947): 3–20.

Lipps, Theodor. "Einfühlung, inner Nachahmung, und Organempfindungen," *Archiv für die gesamte Psychologie* 1 (n.º 1, 1903): 185–204.

Lipps, Theodor. "Zur ästhetischen Mechanik," *Zeitschrift für Ästhetik und Allgemeine Kunstwissenschaft* 1 (1906): 1–29.

Schapiro, Meyer. "Mr. Berenson's values," *Encounter* 16 (enero 1961): 57–65.

Schwartzman, Helen B. "Research on Children's Play: An Overview, and Some Predictions," en *Proceedings of the Association for the Anthropological Study of Play* (1977). Editado por Michael A. Salter. West Point: Leisure Press, 1978. pp. 105–15.

Seerveld, Calvin. *A Christian Critique of Art and Literature* (1964). Toronto: Association for the Advancement of Christian Scholarship, segunda edición, 1977. 127 pp.

Seerveld, Calvin. "A Christian Tin-Can Theory of Man," *Journal of the American Scientific Affiliation* 33 (julio 1981): 74–81.

Seerveld, Calvin. *Rainbows for the Fallen World: Aesthetic Life and Artistic Task*. Toronto: Tuppence Press, 1980. 254 pp.

Sibley, Frank N. "Aesthetic Concepts," *Philosophical Review* 68 (octubre 1959): 421–50. Springer, Sally P. y Georg Deutsch. *Left Brain, Right Brain*. San Francisco: W.H. Freeman & Co., 1981. xii–243.

Steensma, G.J. y Harro W. van Brummelen, eds. *Shaping School Curriculum: A Biblical View*. Terre Haute, Indiana: Signal Publishing Co., 1977. 178 pp.

Tashiro, Tom. "Ambiguity as Aesthetic Principle," en *Dictionary of the History of Ideas*. Nueva York: Charles Scribner's Sons, 1973. 1:48–60.

Wolterstorff, Nicholas. *Art in Action*. Grand Rapids: Wm. B. Eerdmans, 1980. x–240.

Zuidervaart, Lambert. Capítulo 1, "Introduction," en *Kant's Critique of Beauty and Taste: Explorations into a Philosophical Aesthetics*. Toronto: Institute for Christian Studies, tesis de M. Phil., 1977. pp. 1–16.

Notas Finales

1. Traducción propia del griego.

A Call to True, Excellent, and Reformational Making

by Ryan Lauterio

IN TODAY'S RAPIDLY devolving cultural landscape, art and design profoundly influence virtually every aspect of our lives. From the clothes we wear and the cars we drive to the homes we live in, the media we consume, and the stories we read, artistic design impacts our daily existence in countless ways. In this article I argue the importance of art and design from a Christian perspective, urging a robust, reformational approach to these fields that honors Christ and fosters Kingdom flourishing. Every creative endeavor must be carried out under the supreme Lordship of Christ, recognizing His Authority over all aspects of life. Now is the time to reclaim the arts with a sense of truth, excellence, love, compassion, zeal, diligence, and urgency, transforming them into effective reformational expressions of our faith and testaments to the Gospel's transformative power.

The Pervasiveness of Art and Design

Art and design pervade every aspect of our lives, shaping our daily experiences and influencing our choices and values, arresting our affections, shaping our environments and interactions. From the typography that enables us to read to the cartoons our children watch, the films we enjoy, and the aesthetic choices that surround us—artistic influence is everywhere. Finding a facet of life untouched by the power of art and design is nearly impossible. This pervasive nature highlights broadly defined art-making's immense ability to shape culture and society.

Romans 1:20 states, "For his invisible attributes, namely, his eternal power and divine nature, have been clearly perceived, ever since the creation of the world, in the things that have been made. So they are without excuse." While not a direct application, this verse suggests that, as beings made in the image of God, our creations reflect aspects of His divine nature. When the culture we create is demonic and ungodly, it dehumanizes and sows confusion. Conversely, when our culture aims to humanize and align with the teachings of Christ, it reveals glimpses of the Lord's glory. Whether in nature or the objects we create, nothing is neutral; everything has an effect, drawing us closer to or further from the Lord.

The Consequences of Neglect

When art and design are created without a God-given vision, they can become invasive and dehumanizing. We see this in the breakdown of the image of God through sin and brokenness, affecting gender identity, family structure, and the Church's role in society. Poorly executed or visionless art reinforces sin's effects, facilitates further confusion, contributes to societal decay, and glorifies this breakdown as something to be desired. Conversely, when art and design honor God, they enrich our lives, making them richer, truer, and more oriented toward the Kingdom of Heaven. As Proverbs 29:18 says, "Where there is no prophetic vision, the people cast off restraint, but blessed is he who keeps the law." Can there be any doubt at this point that culture-making left in the hands of pagan secularism will continue to drive the options for what we, as Christians, get behind?

Moreover, will the false perception of neutrality continue to capitulate to confusion under the guise of secularist/evolutionary progress? If we as Christians don't make it, the world cannot choose it; we cannot choose it, nor can our children and grandchildren choose it. Moreover, the Lord is not glorified by what we *do not* make. We are, therefore, leaving way too much up to far too many who are dead in their sins and trespasses to define for us what art is, to feed us stories, let alone define what a good story is, and so much more. We must be the ones generating the kind of cool drinks offered to those perishing, and we must do it with confidence in the one whom we serve.

A Call for Reform

Calvin Seerveld, a noted Reformed scholar, aptly stated, "When Christianity abandons the arts, they really do go to hell." The Protestant Church, in particular, has neglected the cultivation of faithful artists for over a century, resulting in a mere imitation of secular culture. To rectify this, we must embark on a multi-generational effort to foster Christian artists who create works that love our neighbors and glorify God. This involves embracing the full spectrum of artistic development, neither replicating medieval aesthetics nor copying contemporary trends, but instead integrating historical and modern artistic knowledge.

Moreover, it involves us chiefly responding to the grace of God, the Lordship of Christ, and the enabling power of the Holy Spirit to make from a grateful heart grace-filled art; art that speaks anew in form and content to the still yet-to-behold wonders of the Lord and His creation that groans eager for the day of salvation. It involves us living humbly, learning to see afresh through the life of Jesus, and what a maker should look like, be like, and focus on; we need to reform what an artist is and take the time and give support to all those who need to develop more excellent skill and theological clarity to do work in visual art, design, craft, film, new media, and more that is saturated with excellence and vision, patience, humility, and prayer infused with a desire to take the time to make well. The Church often struggles to make well and hides behind sentimentality; the time for reform is now. We must train to be excellent.

Embracing Common Grace

Christians must recognize that artistic gifts and knowledge, even outside the Church, remain gifts from God. Just as the Israelites were trained by the Egyptians and received the cities and vineyards of the Canaanites, we, too, must be ready to embrace and redeem the artistic knowledge of the world. Every good thing comes from the Lord, and we should not fear possessing and utilizing these gifts for His glory. Do we believe the Bible? James 1:17 reminds us, "Every good gift and every perfect gift is from above, coming down from the Father of lights with whom there is no variation or shadow due to change." Failing to do so out of fear or disobedience can lead to a barren artistic landscape devoid of the rich cultural contributions we are called to make. We also, however, need to have our eyes open to the crafty and wicked ways of sin, the flesh, and the devil when it comes to art that presents as "angels of light" but is rather there to destroy and devour. Christians who make across the various modalities need deeper spirit-filled discernment and biblical literacy to know what is indeed a good gift and what is meant for evil.

Supporting Christian Artists

The Church must actively support and encourage both young and old artists alike. Art and making are not just for youth, which is a mistake secular society often assumes. It is also not enough to dismiss artistic aspirations as impractical; we must provide theologically sound guidance and practical support to help artists thrive as bold and courageous entrepreneurs of the Kingdom. Churches should nurture artists to be hardworking artisan-makers, committed to their trade, and dedicated to glorifying Christ through their work. This requires a cultural shift within the Church, valuing artistic endeavors as integral to our mission of responsible dominion over creation. As Ephesians 2:10 states, "For we are his workmanship, created in Christ Jesus for good works, which God prepared beforehand, that we should walk in them."

The Necessity of Art in Christian Life

We can see from the Scriptures, art and design are not optional for Christians. We can go back to the garden in Genesis and see dominion-taking presses into every sphere we are called to, and all authority on heaven and earth has been given to the Lord, so how can we not go therefore? Our engagement with the arts should be deliberate and discerning, reflecting the complexity and beauty of the Bible itself. Christian makers and their art should be diverse in style, modality, and purpose, producing a vast array of effects that evoke a wide range of emotions and responses. It should illuminate the glory of creation, the wickedness of sin, the treasure of redemption, and the victory of restoration. Like Jesus, who embodied the perfect image of God, Christian art should sometimes be direct and clear, timely, and lovely in surprising ways and, at other times, challenging and sobering, bold, and unafraid of the criticism of the world which is the same sinful people like you and I who put Jesus on the cross. However, there is no excuse not to be excellent. We must be humble enough to see from history that we can and should be and do more while always pointing toward the truth about God and the world He created.

An Urgent Call to Revival and Reformation

The urgency to do better in the realm of Christian art and design is palpable, yet this effort must be undertaken with a spirit of rest and contentment in the Lord Jesus, recognizing that true cultural change will take time. A deep heart of gratitude is essential for creating the kind of visual artwork we hope to see, as it shifts our motivation from lack or envy to one of thanks, praise, and hopeful, faith-filled obedience. By grounding our artistic endeavors in gratitude and the steadfast love of Christ, we can produce works that truly glorify God and inspire others, cultivating a culture of Truth, Excellence, and Reformation over generations. Let us heed the call of Scripture: "Whatever you do, work heartily, as for the Lord and not for men" (Colossians 3:23). As Christian makers, we have the unique opportunity to lead a revival-like reformation through our creativity reflecting God's glory and advancing His Kingdom on earth. The time is now to reclaim the arts, not as a means to an end but as a powerful expression of our faith and a testament to the transformative power of the Gospel. The world needs Christian artists who can lead by example, shaping the imaginations of God's people and reaching out to those whom God desires to save. As we create with excellence and a reformational spirit, we participate in God's redemptive work, bringing light and beauty into a world desperately in need of both. Let us remember the words of 1 Corinthians 10:31, "So, whether you eat or drink, or whatever you do, do all to the glory of God."

How Then Shall We Make

In conclusion, I exhort us to deeply consider our role and responsibility within the cultural domain of art and design from a distinctly Christian perspective. As we have seen, the pervasive influence of art in shaping culture and the profound implications of engaging within the spheres and modalities of making require not only our attention but also our active, devoted participation. The call to reclaim the arts under the Lordship of Christ is urgent, beckoning the Church to commission Christians afresh, to delve deeply into the sacrificial learning of our crafts, and to embody the truths of Scripture in our artistic endeavors.

How then shall we make? In response to this calling, we must acknowledge our dependence on Christ, recognizing that true creativity and innovation spring from deep, obedient fellowship with Him, not independence from Him. We need the courage to speak the truth through our art, to envision and portray healthy, biblically-founded family structures and proper understandings of maleness and femaleness, especially as this truth flows into the roles men and women are called to as God designed them, which inherently shape our societal spheres and individual roles. This issue of maleness and femaleness is ontological at its core and not arbitrarily assigned as mere role distinctions. There is a pressing need for Christian artists to courageously address and reshape the narratives around gender and sexuality that pervade secular art, narratives often driven by demonic influences that captivate the heart's affections and mislead so many.

Moreover, we must trust in Jesus for the provision only He can bring, steadfastly refusing to compromise with the liberalized leanings that skirt around God's law and selectively engage with Scripture. This approach not only demands a high level of artistic skill and theological depth but also a boldness to stand against the current cultural tides with works that uphold the sanctity of God's design and His commands.

Final Remarks

As we stand at this cultural crossroads, the Church is called not only to support but also to send forth artists who are theologically grounded and skilled, capable of crafting works that reflect the Glory of God and speak of His truth, beauty, and goodness. Let us encourage one another to adopt a reformational mindset that transcends traditional boundaries and explores new territories in art and design. By doing so, we can better serve our communities and witness to the Kingdom in ways that are prophetic, rightly understood, and profoundly so.

In rallying behind this cause, let us also cultivate a spirit of sacrifice, recognizing that the path of a Christian artist is one of continual learning, disciplined practice, and fervent spirit-filled growth. This journey is not for the faint-hearted but for those who dare to impact the world for Christ through the power of creativity and innovation. Thus, may we be inspired to let the Scriptures illuminate our understanding and guide our hands in every creation, knowing that in every line drawn, every color blended, and every form sculpted, we are answering the high yet ordinary calling of our Maker. Through this, may the Church not only commission but also passionately support these endeavors, for in doing so, we are cultivating a legacy of truth, excellence, and transformation that will endure for generations to come to the wonderful praise and Glory of our reigning King Jesus!

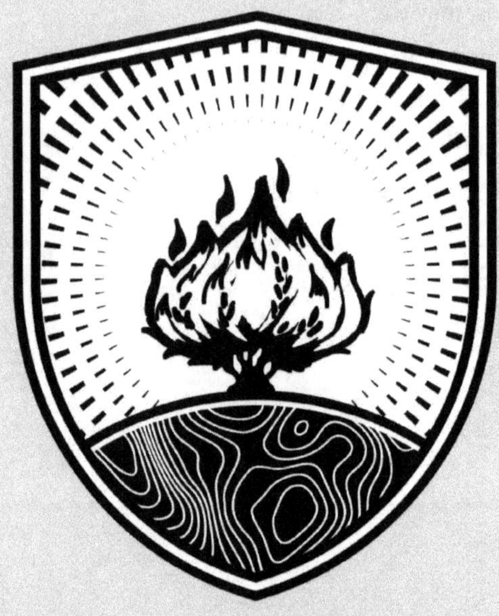

Maker Institute
OF STUDIO ART + THEOLOGY

We develop gospel-gripped, theologically-minded, adept culture makers who faithfully seek to glorify Christ in all things. The fullness of a maker comes forth when the heart, head, and hands are working together in unison.

Our intimate and personal approach includes sound theological training, robust professional and studio practicum, and applied spiritual formation under the guidance of a close-knit community of Christian makers.

Apply Today to Become a Maker Fellow

themakerinstitute.org

Un Llamado a una Obra Verdadera, Excelente y Reformacional

por Ryan Lauterio

E N EL PANORAMA cultural actual, que se degrada rápidamente, el arte y el diseño influyen profundamente en prácticamente todos los aspectos de nuestra vida. Desde la ropa que usamos y los autos que conducimos, hasta los hogares en los que vivimos, los medios que consumimos y las historias que leemos, el diseño artístico impacta nuestra existencia diaria de formas innumerables. En este artículo, argumento la importancia del arte y el diseño desde una perspectiva cristiana, haciendo un llamado a un enfoque reformacional y sólido en estos campos, que honre a Cristo y promueva el florecimiento del Reino. Toda labor creativa debe realizarse bajo el supremo señorío de Cristo, reconociendo Su autoridad sobre todos los aspectos de la vida. Este es el momento de reclamar las artes con un sentido de verdad, excelencia, amor, compasión, celo, diligencia y urgencia, transformándolas en expresiones reformacionales efectivas de nuestra fe y en testimonios del poder transformador del Evangelio.

La Pervasividad del Arte y el Diseño

El arte y el diseño impregnan cada aspecto de nuestras vidas, moldeando nuestras experiencias cotidianas e influyendo en nuestras decisiones, valores, afectos, entornos e interacciones. Desde la tipografía que nos permite leer, hasta las caricaturas que ven nuestros hijos, las películas que disfrutamos y las elecciones estéticas que nos rodean—la influencia artística está en todas partes. Encontrar un ámbito de la vida que no esté tocado por el poder del arte y el diseño es casi imposible. Esta naturaleza omnipresente resalta la inmensa capacidad del arte—entendido en sentido amplio—para formar la cultura y la sociedad.

Romanos 1:20 declara: "Porque las cosas invisibles de él, su eterno poder y deidad, se hacen claramente visibles desde la creación del mundo, siendo entendidas por medio de las cosas hechas, de modo que no tienen excusa." Aunque no se trata de una aplicación directa, este versículo sugiere que, como seres creados a imagen de Dios, nuestras obras reflejan aspectos de Su naturaleza divina. Cuando la cultura que producimos es demoníaca e impía, deshumaniza y siembra confusión. Por el contrario, cuando nuestra cultura busca humanizar y alinearse con las enseñanzas de Cristo, deja entrever destellos de la gloria del Señor. Ya sea en la naturaleza o en los objetos que creamos, nada es neutral; todo tiene un efecto que nos acerca o nos aleja del Señor.

Las Consecuencias del Descuidado

Cuando el arte y el diseño se crean sin una visión dada por Dios, pueden volverse invasivos y deshumanizantes. Esto se manifiesta claramente en la distorsión de la imagen de Dios a causa del pecado y la corrupción, afectando la identidad de género, la estructura familiar y el papel de la Iglesia en la sociedad. El arte mal ejecutado o carente de visión refuerza los efectos del pecado, facilita mayor confusión, contribuye a la decadencia social y glorifica esta descomposición como algo deseable. Por el contrario, cuando el arte y el diseño honran a Dios, enriquecen nuestras vidas, haciéndolas más plenas, más verdaderas y más orientadas hacia el Reino de los Cielos. Como dice Proverbios 29:18: "Sin profecía el pueblo se desenfrena; mas el que guarda la ley es bienaventurado." ¿Acaso queda alguna duda de que, si la creación cultural queda en manos del paganismo secular, continuará moldeando las opciones que tenemos como cristianos?

¿Y acaso seguirá prosperando la falsa percepción de neutralidad, cediendo aún más a la confusión bajo el disfraz del progreso secularista y evolutivo? Si nosotros como cristianos no lo creamos, el mundo no puede elegirlo; nosotros no podemos elegirlo, ni tampoco podrán hacerlo nuestros hijos o nietos. Además, el Señor no es glorificado por aquello que no hacemos. Por tanto, estamos dejando demasiado en manos de quienes están muertos en sus delitos y pecados, permitiéndoles definir lo que es el arte, alimentarnos con historias, e incluso definir lo que constituye una buena historia, entre tantas otras cosas. Debemos ser nosotros quienes generemos esos "vasos de agua fresca" ofrecidos a los que perecen y debemos hacerlo con confianza en Aquel a quien servimos.

Un Llamado a la Reforma

Calvin Seerveld, reconocido académico reformado, dijo con acierto: "Cuando el cristianismo abandona las artes, realmente se van al infierno." La Iglesia protestante, en particular, ha descuidado por más de un siglo la formación de artistas fieles, lo que ha resultado en una mera imitación de la cultura secular. Para corregir esto, debemos emprender un esfuerzo multigeneracional que fomente artistas cristianos que creen obras que amen al prójimo y glorifiquen a Dios. Esto implica abrazar todo el espectro del desarrollo artístico, sin replicar simple-

mente la estética medieval ni copiar las tendencias contemporáneas, sino integrando el conocimiento artístico tanto histórico como moderno.

Asimismo, implica responder primeramente a la gracia de Dios, al señorío de Cristo y al poder capacitador del Espíritu Santo para crear, desde un corazón agradecido, arte lleno de gracia; arte que hable de forma renovada—en forma y contenido—de las maravillas aún por contemplar del Señor y de Su creación, que gime esperando con ansias el día de la redención. Implica vivir con humildad, aprender a ver con ojos renovados a través de la vida de Jesús, y entender cómo debe ser, actuar y enfocarse un verdadero hacedor. Necesitamos reformar lo que entendemos por artista, dedicar tiempo y brindar apoyo a quienes deben desarrollar mayor habilidad y claridad teológica para producir obras en las artes visuales, el diseño, la artesanía, el cine, los nuevos medios y más—obras impregnadas de excelencia, visión, paciencia, humildad y oración, con un deseo profundo de tomarse el tiempo para hacer bien las cosas. La Iglesia con frecuencia lucha por hacer bien las cosas y se refugia en la sentimentalidad; el tiempo para reformar ha llegado. Debemos entrenarnos para alcanzar la excelencia.

Abrazando la Gracia Común

Los cristianos deben reconocer que los dones y conocimientos artísticos, incluso aquellos que se encuentran fuera de la Iglesia, siguen siendo regalos de Dios. Así como los israelitas fueron instruidos por los egipcios y recibieron ciudades y viñedos de los cananeos, nosotros también debemos estar dispuestos a abrazar y redimir el conocimiento artístico del mundo. Todo lo bueno proviene del Señor, y no debemos temer poseer ni utilizar estos dones para Su gloria. ¿Creemos realmente en la Biblia? Santiago 1:17 nos recuerda: "Toda buena dádiva y todo don perfecto desciende de lo alto, del Padre de las luces, en quien no hay mudanza ni sombra de variación." No hacerlo, por temor o desobediencia, puede llevarnos a un panorama artístico árido, privado de las ricas contribuciones culturales que estamos llamados a ofrecer.

Sin embargo, también debemos tener los ojos abiertos ante los caminos astutos y perversos del pecado, la carne y el diablo, especialmente cuando el arte se presenta como "ángel de luz", pero en realidad busca destruir y devorar. Los cristianos que crean en las distintas modalidades artísticas necesitan un discernimiento más profundo, lleno del Espíritu, así como una alfabetización bíblica sólida, para distinguir lo que verdaderamente es un buen don de lo que ha sido concebido para el mal.

Apoyando a los Artistas Cristianos

La Iglesia debe apoyar activamente y animar tanto a jóvenes como a adultos artistas. El arte y la creación no son solo para los jóvenes—un error que la sociedad secular suele asumir. Tampoco basta con descartar las aspiraciones artísticas como poco prácticas; debemos ofrecer una guía teológicamente sólida y un apoyo práctico que permita a los artistas prosperar como emprendedores valientes del Reino. Las iglesias deben formar artistas que sean artesanos diligentes, comprometidos con su oficio y dedicados a glorificar a Cristo a través de su trabajo. Esto requiere un cambio cultural dentro de la Iglesia, valorando el quehacer artístico como parte integral de nuestra misión de ejercer dominio responsable sobre la creación. Como dice Efesios 2:10: "Porque somos hechura suya, creados en Cristo Jesús para buenas obras, las cuales Dios preparó de antemano para que anduviésemos en ellas."

La Necesidad del Arte en la Vida Cristiana

Las Escrituras dejan claro que el arte y el diseño no son opcionales para los cristianos. Podemos remontarnos al jardín del Edén en Génesis y ver cómo el mandato de ejercer dominio se extiende a cada esfera a la que hemos sido llamados. Toda autoridad en el cielo y en la tierra ha sido dada al Señor, ¿cómo entonces no habríamos de ir? Nuestra participación en las artes debe ser deliberada y discernida, reflejando la complejidad y belleza de la propia Biblia. Los hacedores cristianos y su arte deben ser diversos en estilo, modalidad y propósito, produciendo una vasta gama de efectos que evoquen una amplia variedad de emociones y respuestas. Su labor debe iluminar la gloria de la creación, la maldad del pecado, el tesoro de la redención y la victoria de la restauración.

Así como Jesús encarnó la imagen perfecta de Dios, el arte cristiano debe, a veces, ser directo y claro, oportuno y hermoso de maneras sorprendentes, y en otras ocasiones, desafiante y sobrio, valiente y sin temor a la crítica del mundo —ese mismo mundo pecador, como tú y yo, que llevó a Jesús a la cruz. Sin embargo, no hay excusa para no buscar la excelencia. Debe-

mos tener la humildad suficiente para aprender de la historia que podemos y debemos ser y hacer más, siempre apuntando a la verdad acerca de Dios y del mundo que Él creó.

Un Llamado Urgente al Avivamiento y la Reforma

La urgencia de hacer mejor las cosas en el ámbito del arte y el diseño cristiano es palpable, pero este esfuerzo debe emprenderse con un espíritu de descanso y contentamiento en el Señor Jesús, reconociendo que el verdadero cambio cultural tomará tiempo. Un corazón profundamente agradecido es esencial para crear el tipo de arte visual que anhelamos ver, pues cambia nuestra motivación de la carencia o la envidia a una de gratitud, alabanza y obediencia esperanzada y llena de fe. Al fundamentar nuestras obras artísticas en la gratitud y en el amor constante de Cristo, podemos producir creaciones que verdaderamente glorifiquen a Dios e inspiren a otros, cultivando una cultura de Verdad, Excelencia y Reforma a lo largo de generaciones.

Prestemos atención al llamado de la Escritura: "Y todo lo que hagáis, hacedlo de corazón, como para el Señor y no para los hombres" (Col. 3:23). Como hacedores cristianos, tenemos la oportunidad única de liderar una reforma semejante a un avivamiento mediante nuestra creatividad, reflejando la gloria de Dios y avanzando Su Reino en la tierra. Ha llegado la hora de reclamar las artes, no como un simple medio para lograr fines, sino como una expresión poderosa de nuestra fe y como testimonio del poder transformador del Evangelio. El mundo necesita artistas cristianos que lideren con el ejemplo, moldeando la imaginación del pueblo de Dios y alcanzando a aquellos que Él desea salvar.

Al crear con excelencia y un espíritu reformacional, participamos en la obra redentora de Dios, trayendo luz y belleza a un mundo desesperadamente necesitado de ambas. Recordemos las palabras de 1 Corintios 10:31: "Si, pues, coméis o bebéis, o hacéis otra cosa, hacedlo todo para la gloria de Dios."

¿Cómo, Pues, Debemos Crear?

En conclusión, exhorto a que consideremos profundamente nuestro papel y responsabilidad dentro del dominio cultural del arte y el diseño desde una perspectiva distintivamente cristiana. Como hemos visto, la influencia omnipresente del arte en la formación de la cultura y las profundas implicaciones de participar en los diversos ámbitos y modalidades del hacer re-

quieren no solo nuestra atención, sino también nuestra participación activa y devota. El llamado a reclamar las artes bajo el señorío de Cristo es urgente; la Iglesia debe volver a comisionar a los cristianos a sumergirse en el aprendizaje sacrificial de sus oficios y a encarnar las verdades de las Escrituras en sus esfuerzos artísticos.

¿Cómo, pues, debemos crear? En respuesta a este llamado, debemos reconocer nuestra dependencia de Cristo, sabiendo que la verdadera creatividad e innovación brotan de una comunión profunda y obediente con Él, no de una independencia de Él. Necesitamos el valor para hablar la verdad a través de nuestro arte, para imaginar y representar estructuras familiares saludables y fundadas bíblicamente, así como una comprensión adecuada de la masculinidad y la feminidad, especialmente en cuanto estas verdades fluyen hacia los roles que hombres y mujeres están llamados a desempeñar según el diseño de Dios, el cual moldea inherentemente nuestras esferas sociales y funciones individuales.

Este asunto de la masculinidad y la feminidad es ontológico en su esencia, no una simple asignación arbitraria de roles. Existe una necesidad urgente de que los artistas cristianos aborden con valentía y reformen las narrativas en torno al género y la sexualidad que dominan el arte secular—narrativas con frecuencia impulsadas por influencias demoníacas que cautivan los afectos del corazón y desvían a muchos.

Además, debemos confiar en Jesús para la provisión que solo Él puede dar, rehusándonos firmemente a transigir con las tendencias liberalizadas que evaden la ley de Dios y se relacionan selectivamente con las Escrituras. Este enfoque exige no solo un alto nivel de destreza artística y profundidad teológica, sino también una valentía firme para resistir las corrientes culturales actuales mediante obras que afirmen la santidad del diseño de Dios y de Sus mandamientos.

Palabras Finales

Al encontrarnos en esta encrucijada cultural, la Iglesia está llamada no solo a apoyar, sino también a enviar a artistas que estén bien arraigados teológicamente y capacitados técnicamente, capaces de crear obras que reflejen la gloria de Dios y proclamen Su verdad, Su belleza y Su bondad. Animémonos mutuamente a adoptar una mentalidad reformacional que trascienda los límites tradicionales y explore nuevos territorios en el arte y el diseño. Al hacerlo, podremos servir mejor a nues-

tras comunidades y dar testimonio del Reino de maneras que sean proféticas, bien entendidas y profundamente transformadoras.

Al unirnos en esta causa, cultivemos también un espíritu de sacrificio, reconociendo que el camino del artista cristiano es uno de aprendizaje continuo, práctica disciplinada y crecimiento ferviente lleno del Espíritu. Este viaje no es para los pusilánimes, sino para aquellos que se atreven a impactar el mundo para Cristo mediante el poder de la creatividad y la innovación. Que las Escrituras iluminen nuestro entendimiento y guíen nuestras manos en cada creación, sabiendo que en cada línea trazada, cada color mezclado y cada forma esculpida, estamos respondiendo al alto y, sin embargo, ordinario llamado de nuestro Creador.

Así, que la Iglesia no solo comisione, sino que también apoye con pasión estos esfuerzos, porque al hacerlo estamos cultivando un legado de verdad, excelencia y transformación que perdurará por generaciones, para alabanza maravillosa y gloria de nuestro Rey reinante: ¡Jesús!

AUTHORS

STEVEN R. MARTINS

Steven is the founding director of the Cántaro Institute and founding pastor of Sevilla Chapel in St. Catharines. He holds a Master's degree *summa cum laude* in Theological Studies with a focus on Christian apologetics from Veritas International University (Santa Ana, CA., USA) and a Bachelor of Human Resource Management from York University (Toronto, ON., Canada). He is the General Editor of *The Old Spanish Reformers* series, has translated several sixteenth-century works of the Spanish protestant reformers, has authored and coedited numerous books, including *Apologetics: Studies in Biblical Apologetics for a Christian Worldview*, *Lectures on Reformation & Culture*, and *La Fuente: Iberoamerican Journal for Christian Worldview*, and has contributed several articles to journals and periodicals. Steven is married to Cindy and they live in the region of Niagara with their children Matthias, Timothy, Nehemías, and Raquel.

RYAN ERAS

Ryan serves as Headmaster of Niagara Classical Academy, where he also teaches Math and P.E. He earned a BA in History and an MI in Library and Information Science. Ryan and his wife Rachel were involved in the founding and operation of Westminster Classical Christian Academy in Toronto, and the early founding of Oak Hill Academy in Hamilton. They also founded the Wolf's Head House, providing adults foundational training from a robustly Christian perspective so they can lead and train the younger generation and shape culture to the glory of God. Since moving to the Niagara region in 2018, they and their five children have been blessed to be able to participate in the classical and Christian vision for education in both homeschool and day school settings. Ryan is an elder at White Stone Church of Christ and enjoys cooking, weightlifting, and trying to learn to sing harmony.

CALVIN G. SEERVELD

Seerveld was born in 1930 in Long Island, New York, and was shaped by his Calvinist upbringing and early work in his family's market, calling himself "a fishmonger's son." His mother, a musician and former legal secretary, nurtured his love for the arts, leading to his study of music, literature, and philosophy. After earning degrees from Calvin College and the University of Michigan, Seerveld pursued doctoral studies in philosophy and comparative literature at the Free University of Amsterdam, with interim studies in Basel and Rome. Fluent in several languages, he married Inès Naudin ten Cate in 1956. In 1959, Seerveld became one of the founding professors at Trinity Christian College, shaping its philosophy department and curriculum with a deep integration of faith, scholarship, and cultural engagement. His lectures, chapel talks, and oratorio translations of biblical texts like Song of Songs and Ecclesiastes left a lasting impression. In 1973, he joined the Institute for Christian Studies in Toronto and continued to publish extensively, including *A Christian Critique of Art and Literature*, *Voicing God's Psalms*, and *Tough Stuff from the Bible*. Seerveld and Inès also established the Calvin and Inès Seerveld Arts in Society Fund at Trinity, which has supported major art projects and will continue to do so for years to come. His enduring legacy reflects a lifelong commitment to Reformational thought, the arts, and the lordship of Christ in all of life.

RYAN LAUTERIO

Ryan is a multi-award-winning studio artist, educator, and founder whose life and work are devoted to the intersection of art, theology, and aesthetics under the Lordship of Christ. He is a founder and CEO of The Maker Institute of Studio Art and Theology, a 501(c)(3), and a founder of Made Makers: Christian Art and Design Education, a K–12, biblically integrated curriculum and online streaming platform for homeschool and Christian school communities. Ryan holds a B.A. ('03) and M.A. ('05) in Studio Art from CSU Sacramento and an M.F.A. ('09) in Painting and Printmaking from Virginia Commonwealth University (VCU). From 2007 to 2024, Ryan served as Assistant Professor and Drawing Studio Area Head in the Art Foundation Program at VCUarts, one of the nation's top-ranked public art schools. Ryan is also the founder and Director of Shockoe Artspace, a contemporary art gallery he launched in 2011 in partnership with Remnant Church and formalized as a 501(c)(3) in 2016. His studio work has been exhibited nationally and internationally, is part of private and corporate collections including Capital One, and has been published in New American Paintings, Image Journal, and more. His visual and written work is also featured in *A Prophet in the Darkness: Exploring Theology in the Art of Georges Rouault* (IVP, Studies in Theology and the Arts). Ryan and his wife Laura are homeschool parents to three children (with one on the way) and are faithful members of Remnant Church in Richmond, VA.